THE
SHAKESPEARE
COMPANION

Emma Jones and Rhiannon Guy

A THINK BOOK FOR

ROBSON BOOKS

The Birdwatcher's Companion
by Malcolm Tait and Olive Tayler

The Cook's Companion
by Jo Swinnerton

The Countryside Companion
by Malcolm Tait and Olive Tayler

The Fishing Companion
by Lesley Crawford

The Gardener's Companion
by Vicky Bamforth

The Golfer's Companion
by Chris Martin

The History of Britain Companion
by Jo Swinnerton

The Ideas Companion
by Johnny Acton

The Legal Companion
by Vincent Powell

The Literary Companion
by Emma Jones

The London Companion
by Jo Swinnerton

The Moviegoer's Companion
by Rhiannon Guy

The Politics Companion
Edited by Daisy Sampson

The Sailing Companion
by Miles Kendall

The Shakespeare Companion
by Emma Jones and Rhiannon Guy

The Traveller's Companion
by Georgina Newbery and Rhiannon Guy

The Walker's Companion
by Malcolm Tait

The Wildlife Companion
by Malcolm Tait and Olive Tayler

SERIES EDITORS

Malcolm Tait, Emma Jones, Jo Swinnerton
and Rhiannon Guy

Take, then, this your companion by the hand,
Who hath a story ready for your ear.

Measure for Measure, Act IV, scene i

THINK

A Think Book
for Robson Books

First published in Great Britain in 2005 by
Robson Books
The Chrysalis Building, Bramley Road, London W10 6SP

An imprint of **Chrysalis** Books Group plc

Edited by Emma Jones and Rhiannon Guy
Companion team: Tilly Boulter, James Collins, Lou Millward,
Matt Packer, Sonja Patel, Jo Swinnerton and Malcolm Tait

Think Publishing
The Pall Mall Deposit
124-128 Barlby Road, London W10 6BL
www.thinkpublishing.co.uk

ISBN 1-86105-913-2

Printed in Italy

I thank God for William Shakespeare.
An extraordinary, superhuman genius...
Where did he get all that knowledge? Where
did all that wisdom come from? If you go
through all the plays you find that he knew
something about everything. He had a phrase
or a sentence, a word for every conceivable
human situation and emotion.

Sir Derek Jacobi

A STANDING OVATION TO

This book would not have been possible without the determined research, inspired ideas, and dogged support of:

Tania Adams, Moa Bejersten, Amshula Ghumman, Angharad, Douglas and Kay Guy, Anthony, Diane, Dominic, Katie and Rachel Jones, Marek Handzel, Hazel Mendonca, Nick Kimber, Naomi Pollard, Lindsey Russell and Toby Wagstaff.

INTRODUCTION

Even though the hard facts we know about Shakespeare do not amount to much more than a rhyming couplet, an immense scholarship around the playwright has sprung up over the last four hundred years. This book does not weigh-in on that scholarly debate, nor does it provide an exam revision guide, but it does ask and answer the questions that you didn't even know you needed the answer for, such as: Was Shakespeare a freemason? How many *Star Trek* episodes did the Bard inspire? What is a 'Lipsbury Pinfold'? Which character has the most lines? And, what would you get if you introduced Homer Simpson to *Macbeth*?

Not simply the fodder of secondary school English lessons, William Shakespeare has inspired a lot of people to do some pretty great things over the years – and some pretty weird and silly things too. This book celebrates everything about Shakespeare. His history and his histories, and his tragedies, comedies and poetry are all waiting for you in these pages.

Rhiannon Guy, Editor

Comedies

All's Well That Ends Well
As You Like It
The Comedy of Errors
Cymbeline
Love's Labour's Lost
Measure for Measure
The Merry Wives of Windsor
The Merchant of Venice
A Midsummer-Night's Dream
Much Ado About Nothing
Pericles, Prince of Tyre
The Taming of the Shrew
The Tempest
Troilus and Cressida
Twelfth Night; or What You Will
The Two Gentlemen of Verona
The Winter's Tale

Histories

King Henry IV, Part One
King Henry IV, Part Two
King Henry V
King Henry VI, Part One
King Henry VI, Part Two
King Henry VI, Part Three
King Henry VIII
King John
King Richard II
King Richard III

Tragedies

Antony and Cleopatra
Coriolanus
Hamlet, Prince of Denmark
Julius Caesar
King Lear
Macbeth
Othello, The Moor of Venice
Romeo and Juliet
Timon of Athens
Titus Andronicus

10 *Percentage of a worker's daily wage needed to buy a standing room ticket for the original Globe theatre*

The Globe theatre was built c.1598 in London's Bankside district, on the South Bank of the Thames. However, the building actually began its life much earlier on the North Bank, in Shoreditch, when it was known simply as 'The Theatre' (built 1576). Its move across the river began around 1597 when, popular legend has it, the lease of land on which it was situated was due to expire. Worried that the building would be destroyed, owner Richard Burbage organised for it to be dismantled, transported across the river, and rebuilt as the Globe.

The theatre took one year to rebuild and began its first season in its new location in 1599. The theatre was octagonal and sat (and stood) 3,000 spectators over three storeys. The plays were performed on a rectangular stage platform measuring approximately 44 feet wide and 28 feet deep.

On 29 June 1613, during a performance of *King Henry VIII*, the theatre burned to the ground after a stray spark from a canon set the thatched roof alight. Although it was rebuilt by 1614, it faced opposition from the Puritans, and suffered the fate of London's other theatres, closing down in 1642, before being razed in 1644 to make room for housing.

Thanks to the determination of American actor, Sam Wanamaker, the Globe theatre rose from the ashes and opened its doors to the public once more in 1997, just 200 yards away from the building of 1599. A careful reconstruction of the 1599 theatre, the present-day Globe theatre was the first thatched-roof building to have been permitted in London since the Great Fire of London in 1666. It managed to side-step the rules by adding sprinklers to the roof to protect it from fire. It continues to stage Shakespeare's plays in the summer months.

SHOWING HIS FACE

A brew with the Bard

Anyone who had popped in for a pint in Shakespeare's home county of Warwickshire in the nineteenth century would have recognised a familiar face. Flower's Breweries, founded in 1830, used an image of Shakespeare, loosely based on the Shakespeare Bust in Stratford-upon-Avon's Holy Trinity Church, as the trademark of its Flower's Ale. It wasn't the only erudite ale to emerge in the nineteenth century; Pale East India Ale and Extra Stout Porter – both produced in Stratford-upon-Avon – used images of Shakespeare on their labels.

The Campaign for Real Ale (CAMRA) has continued the theme into the twenty-first century. Supporters of the Stratford Branch receive a quarterly newsletter entitled 'ShakesBeer', alerting them to CAMRA events and pub recommendations in the area.

THE END OF THE STORY

Like much of Shakespeare's life, little is known about Shakespeare's death on 23 April 1616, but a diary entry by local vicar and family-friend John Ward offers one possible explanation. Ward wrote that Shakespeare and fellow poets Michael Drayton and Ben Jonson 'had a merry meeting, and it seems drank too hard, for Shakespeare died of a fever there contracted'. However, this account of Shakespeare's drunken demise has been much disputed. Ward made the diary entry 50 years after Shakespeare's death.

POETIC PUZZLERS

Which of the following is the odd one out?
Ephesus • Alexandria
Messina • Coventry
Answer on page 153.

A PLAY TO DIE FOR

Rumours of the 'curse of *Macbeth*' have been traced as far back as the play's opening night on 7 August 1606, when the boy actor playing Lady Macduff collapsed and died, apparently forcing Shakespeare to play the role. Since then, productions all over the world have suffered from severe doses of bad luck – some even resulting in death. In 1672 it was fatal for the actor playing Duncan, for the actor playing Macbeth had substituted the false dagger with a real blade, stabbing him to death in full view of the audience. A second actor, Harold Norman, died in 1947, also stabbed with a real blade. And in an 1849 performance in New York's Astor Palace, the audience suffered too; the play ended in a riot, killing more than 20 audience members and injuring hundreds.

The superstition was given yet more credence in 1937, when during a production at the Old Vic, a 25-pound weight crashed within an inch of Laurence Olivier, the actor playing Macbeth. It wasn't the only bad luck to strike the production's run; both the director and the actress playing Lady Macduff were involved in a car accident on the way to the theatre, and the theatre's grande dame Lilian Bayliss died of a heart attack on the day of the dress rehearsal.

Other actors said to have suffered from or witnessed the curse in action include Charlton Heston, who suffered severe burns to his groin and leg from tights accidentally soaked in kerosene; actress Sybil Thorndyke, who was nearly strangled by another member of the cast while playing Lady Macbeth; and Paul Scofield, Orson Welles and Stanislavski.

Blackadder: [punches Shakespeare]
*That is for every schoolboy and schoolgirl for the next 400 years.
Have you any idea how much suffering you're going to cause?
Hours spent at school desks trying to find 'one' joke in*
A Midsummer-Night's Dream. *Wearing stupid tights in school
plays saying things like, 'What ho, my Lord,' and, 'Oh, look,
here comes Othello talking total crap as usual.'*

SHAKESPEARE'S SIGNATURES

**Only six instances of Shakespeare's signature survive today. They
can be found on:**

A 1612 deposition – *William Shackper*
A 1612 Blackfriar's deed – *William Shakspear*
A 1612 Blackfriars' mortgage – *William Shakpea*
His will, page one – *William Shacksere*
His will, page two – *Willm. Shakspere*
His will, page three – *William Shakespeare*

WRITERS ON WILLIAM

The plays of William Shakespeare were written on the playing fields of Eton. Or, at least, the plays of Shakespeare as they have been taught in school, were. In the form in which most people first encounter them, *Hamlet* or *Macbeth*, *King Lear* or *Othello* are made to seem as if they have very little to do with the theatre, with the seventeenth century, with a man trying to create new rituals for a world that was changing at a frightening pace, and everything to do with building character, with the nineteenth century, with teaching us lessons about how we should behave. They are the mental equivalent of a cold shower; shocking, awful, but in some obscure way good for you, bracing you for the terrors of life and keeping you mind off bad thoughts about politics, society and the way the world changes. They are an ordeal after which you're supposed to feel better, a kind of mental museli that cleans out the system and purges the soul. And, like museli, they are boring, fruity and full of indigestible roughage.

The plays that Shakespeare actually wrote, on the other hand, are full of great stories, extraordinary people, wonderfully rich language and skill with drama that has seldom been matched.

**Fintan O'Toole,
*Shakespeare is Hard,
but so is Life***

Numerous forgeries and supposed spitting images of Shakespeare have appeared over the years, including the 'Sanders Portrait' (above), discovered in Canada in 2001. The find caused something of a stir among enthusiasts searching for an authentic portrait of the playwright, for the painting had a label attached to the back which read, 'Shakspere, born April 23 1564, died April 23 1616, aged 52, this likeness taken 1603, age at that time 39 years.'

Tests carried out on the portrait verified the claim that the painting was indeed from the seventeenth century, and a scene painter from Shakespeare's theatre company, named John Sanders, was suggested as the painter. But, despite this authentication, most scholars are sceptical that it is a true portrait. Not only does he look younger than his supposed 39 years, but the portrait itself is markedly different from the other Shakespeare likenesses painted at the time.

AT HOME WITH SHAKESPEARE

Now considered one of Britain's most important historic buildings, Shakespeare's Birthplace in Stratford-upon-Avon owes its preservation to the legendary American showman Phineas Taylor Barnum (dubbed 'The Shakespeare of Advertising' for his success at drawing crowds). On a trip to England in the 1850s, Barnum found the cottage in a state of disrepair and attempted to buy it and ship it brick-by-brick to the US for display in his museum. This stirred the horrified Stratfordians into action and the Shakespeare Birthday Committee (the forerunner of the Shakespeare Birthplace Trust) was established to raise the £3,000 needed to save and restore the house.

NOT A FAN

'With the single exception of Homer, there is no eminent writer, not even Sir Walter Scott, whom I can despise so entirely as I despise Shakespeare when I measure my mind against his', once wrote George Bernard Shaw. 'The intensity of my impatience occasionally reaches such a pitch, that it would positively be a relief for me to dig him up and throw stones at him.'

Shaw was equally scathing toward Shakespeare's adoring fans. He deemed them 'foolish bardolaters', wrote pitifully of 'bardolatrous' audiences, and coined the now popular term 'bardolatry', in order to sarcastically describe the obsessive study of the playwright's work.

It's probably safe to say he wouldn't be a fan of this book.

QUOTE UNQUOTE

Fantastic! And it was all written with a feather!
Said to be uttered by Samuel Goldwyn, film producer,
on first looking through Shakespeare's plays

A ROYAL SEAL OF APPROVAL

Queen Elizabeth I (reigned 1558-1603)

Legend has it that an 11-year-old William received his first taste of court life when watching the pageantry associated with Queen Elizabeth's visit to Kenilworth Castle near Stratford-upon-Avon in 1572. It is thought that this formed the basis for many of the regal scenes in his plays, while the time he spent in Queen Elizabeth I's Court (performing in the Lord Chamberlain's Men), filled in the gap.

As part of the Lord Chamberlain's Men, Shakespeare performed in front of Elizabeth at least 31 times in the last 10 years of her reign, that's compared to the 37 performances notched up by rival companies between them. Ben Jonson certainly felt she was a fan; in his dedication to Shakespeare in the First Folio, he wrote:

> *Sweet Swan of Avon! What a sight it were*
> *To see thee in our waters yet appear*
> *And make those flights upon the banks of Thames,*
> *That so did take Eliza, and our James.*

Nicholas Rowe, in his *Life of Shakespeare* (1709), reports that the Queen was particularly 'well pleased with that admirable character of Falstaff' (by that time killed off in *King Henry V*) and that she 'commanded him to continue it for one play more, and to show him in love'. Shakespeare duly did so, in *The Merry Wives of Windsor*.

Shakespeare created some of literature's most memorable scoundrels...

Iago – Lying, cheating, lust-driven backstabber in *Othello*.

King Richard III – Self-pitying sociopath driven to murder by kingly ambition.

Cornwall – Malicious schemer who gouges out the Earl of Gloucester's eyes in *King Lear*.

Aaron the Moor – Treacherous mastermind of murder and rape in *Titus Andronicus*.

Edmund – Vindictive plotter who strives to destroy his brother and father in *King Lear*.

Lady Macbeth – Ruthless, overpowering instigator of her husband's murderous actions.

Claudius – Hamlet's unscrupulous uncle who uses treachery and murder to fulfill his ambitions.

Regan and Goneril – Cruel and pitiless daughters of King Lear.

Angelo – Wicked opportunist who attempts to use his power to bed Isabella in *Measure for Measure*.

Bertram – Unreliable cad who refuses to honour his husbandry duties in *All's Well That Ends Well* until he is forced to do so by his wife's cunning.

WRITERS ON WILLIAM

Among the many reasons which make me glad to have been born in England, one of the first is that I read Shakespeare in my mother tongue. If I try to imagine myself as one who cannot know him face to face, who hears him only speaking from afar, and that in accents which only through the labouring intelligence can touch the living soul, there comes upon me a sense of chill discouragement, of dreary deprivation. I am wont to think that I can read Homer, and, assuredly, if any man enjoys him, it is I; but can I for a moment dream that Homer yields me all his music, that his word is to me as to him who walked by the Hellenic shore where Hellas lived? I know that there reaches me across the vast of time no more than a faint and broken echo; I know that it would be fainter still, but for its blending with those memories of youth which are as a glimmer of the world's primeval glory. Let every land have joy of its poet; for the poet is the land itself, all its greatness and its sweetness, all that incommunicable heritage for which men live and die.

George Gissing, *The Private Papers of Henry Ryecroft*

*Cut the crap, Hamlet! My biological clock is
ticking, and I want babies 'now'!*
Ophelia, in the Reduced Shakespeare Company's
Complete Works of William Shakespeare (Abridged)

THE LOST PLAYS

Cardenio

When the Globe theatre burned to the ground on 29 June 1613, it is thought to have taken with it the only remaining copy of *Cardenio*, one of Shakespeare's 'lost plays'. Known to have been performed at least once by the King's Men (Shakespeare's theatre company), the play is thought to have been authored by Shakespeare and fellow playwright, John Fletcher.

The earliest mention of the play comes from the accounts of the treasurer to King James, Lord Stanhope, which records a sum of money paid on 20 May 1613, for a play called 'Cardano' or 'Cardenno'. The payment was collected by John Heminge, a member of the King's Men, and one of the actors who prepared and oversaw the First Folio edition of Shakespeare's plays.

In 1728, editor and author Lewis Theobold claimed to have obtained three Restoration-era manuscripts of an unnamed play by Shakespeare, which he edited, 'improved', and released as *Double Falsehood*. It depicts the tragicomic story of Cardenio, a character who first appeared in Cervantes' *Don Quixote*. But while Theobold's play still survives, his manuscript copies of the Shakespeare play, on which he supposedly based his work, were themselves destroyed in an 1808 fire at the Covent Garden Playhouse.

But the story doesn't end there. In 1990, a handwriting expert by the name of Charles Hamilton re-examined a 1611 manuscript entitled *The Second Maiden's Tragedy*, identifying it as the missing *Cardenio* but with the characters presented under different names. Although it was previously attributed to Thomas Middleton, the play has since been performed and published as Shakespeare's *Cardenio*. However, it is an attribution greatly disputed by experts on Shakespeare.

HEAD FIRST

Although commonly associated with the Queen in *Alice's Adventures in Wonderland*, the phrase 'off with his head' actually originated in Shakespeare's *King Richard III* (Act III, scene iv). Richard of Gloucestershire (as he was then) sentences Lord Hastings to death with the words: 'Thou art a traitor: off with his head.'

AN OPERATIC TWIST

The Tempest – Henry Purcell (1690)

Otello – Gioacchino Rossini (1816)

Das Liebesverbot – Richard Wagner (1836)
based on *Measure for Measure*

Macbeth – Giuseppe Verdi (1847)

Die lustigen Weiber von Windsor – Carl Otto Nicolai (1849)
based on *The Merry Wives of Windsor*

La Tempesta – Jacques Halévy (1850)

Béatrice et Bénédict – Hector Berlioz (1862)
based on *Much Ado About Nothing*

Roméo et Juliette – Charles Gounod (1867)

Hamlet – Ambroise Thomas (1868)

Otello – Giuseppe Verdi (1887)

Falstaff – Giuseppe Verdi (1893)
based on *The Merry Wives of Windsor*

Troilus and Cressida – William Walton (1947-1954)

A Midsummer Night's Dream – Benjamin Britten (1960)

Antony and Cleopatra – Samuel Barber (1966)

THERE ARE NO SMALL PARTS
ONLY SMALL ACTORS

Six small parts to challenge the biggest actor...

Role: Second Senator
Total no. of words: One
Line: 'Ay'
Cymbeline, Act III, scene vii

Role: Second Soldier
Total no. of words: Two
Line: 'Nor I.'
Coriolanus, Act I, scene iv

Role: Third Soldier
Total no. of words: One
Line: 'Stand!'
Julius Caesar, Act IV, scene ii

Role: Philip
Total no. of words: Three
Line: 'How now, Grumio!'
The Taming of the Shrew,
Act IV, scene i

Role: Taurus
Total no. of words: Two
Line: 'My Lord?'
Antony and Cleopatra,
Act III, scene viii

Role: Second Pirate
Total no. of words: Four
Line: 'A prize! a prize!' *Pericles*,
Prince of Tyre, Act IV, scene i

'A ship at sea; afterwards an uninhabited island' opens *The Tempest* (c.1611-12) as a storm strikes the characters' ship. But while no source has been discovered for Shakespeare's characters, his story had its roots in reality, for the tale is thought to have been inspired by the shipwreck of British Admiral Sir George Somers in 1609. Somers had been en route to America when a hurricane struck his ship, Sea-Adventure, depositing him off the coast of Bermuda, which he 'claimed' for Britain. Several accounts of the wreck and the surviving crew were rushed into print in 1610 including *A Discovery of the Bermudas* by Sylvester Jourdain and William Strachey's *True Repertory of the Wracke*, both of which supplied details for the storm as described by Shakespeare.

WHAT IS SHAKESPEARE'S MOST USED WORD?

The 10 most frequent words used by the author in *The Complete Works of Shakespeare*:

	Word	Frequency
1.	the	27,457
2.	and	26,285
3.	I	21,206
4.	to	19,938
5.	of	17,079
6.	a	14,679
7.	you	14,326
8.	my	13,075
9.	that	11,725
10.	in	11,511

Later down the list appears the first infinitive verb, 'be' (7,418), the first noun, 'love' (2,291), and the first name, 'Henry' (1,026). 'Death' (961) is slightly more popular than 'life' (924), but 'love' (2,291) manages to trump 'hate' (186).

WHAT'S THE PROBLEM?

Commonly known as Shakespeare's 'problem plays', *All's Well That Ends Well, Measure for Measure*, and *Troilus and Cressida* have frustrated scholars for centuries because they do not fit neatly into the usual categories of comedy, tragedy or history. Critic FS Boas coined the term in *Shakespeare and His Predecessors* (1896). He felt that the plays were problems to classify because they lacked the usual final-act conclusion of themes and debates.

Age of Shakespeare on the birth of his first daughter, just six months after
his wedding

MOST LINES FOR A LADY

The five female parts with the most lines:

Part	Number of lines
Rosalind *(As You Like It)*	685
Cleopatra *(Antony and Cleopatra)*	678
Imogen *(Cymbeline)*	594
Portia *(The Merchant of Venice)*	574
Juliet *(Romeo and Juliet)*	542

The average length of a major female role in Shakespeare is 410 lines.

QUOTE UNQUOTE

Alive today he would undoubtedly have written and directed motion pictures, plays and God knows what. Instead of saying 'This medium is not good,' he would have used it and made it good. If some people called some of his work cheap (which some of it is), he wouldn't have cared a rap, because he would know that without some vulgarity there is no complete man.
Raymond Chandler, American author

WRITERS ON WILLIAM

Terrible poet or deliberate satirist? Critics are divided when it comes to the poetry of William Topaz McGonagall (1825–1902)...

Immortal! William Shakespeare, there's none can you excel,
You have drawn out your characters remarkably well,
Which is delightful for to see enacted upon the stage
For instance, the love-sick Romeo, or Othello, in a rage;
His writings are a treasure, which the world cannot repay,
He was the greatest poet of the past or of the present day
Also the greatest dramatist, and is worthy of the name,
I'm afraid the world shall never look upon his like again.
His tragedy of Hamlet is moral and sublime,
And for purity of language, nothing can be more fine
For instance, to hear the fair Ophelia making her moan,
At her father's grave, sad and alone

...Immortal! Bard of Avon, your writings are divine,
And will live in the memories of you admirers until the end of time;
Your plays are read in family circles with wonder and delight,
While seated around the fireside on a cold winter's night.
William Topaz McGonagall, *An Address to Shakespeare*

20 *Price, in pounds sterling, of a Shakespeare teapot in the Historic Royal Palaces shop*

*Macbeth always thought that there was
something vaguely creepy about his wife...*

THE LOST PLAYS

Love's Labour's Won

Francis Meres, praising some of Shakespeare's comedies in his
Palladis Tamia, Wits Treasury of 1598, speaks of *Two Gentlemen of
Verona, The Comedy of Errors, Love's Labour's Lost, A Midsummer-
Night's Dream, The Merchant of Venice* and *Love's Labour's Won*. But
even though it was in wide usage at the time, no copy of this last play
remains – or does it?

Generally recognised as a sequel to *Love's Labour's Lost* (which ends
with a suggestion of the marriages to come), this 'lost play' could simply
be an alternative title for a comedy we now know by another name (and
not listed by Meres). *The Taming of the Shrew* was the popular choice
until 1953, but the discovery of a 1603 catalogue listing both the plays
soon put an end to that theory. The play has since been linked to *Much
Ado About Nothing* and *All's Well That Ends Well*.

John Barrymore performed Hamlet 101 times in the 1922 theatre season in New York. Lawrence Olivier said of his performance at the Sam H Harris Theatre: 'Everything about him was exciting. He was athletic, he had charisma, and, to my young mind, he played the part to perfection.'

Kenneth Branagh's 1996 film version was the first to use the play's full text. It lasted four hours and two minutes.

Richard Burbage played Hamlet in the very first production. Weighing in at nearly 17 stone, he may not have had the look we associate with the role today, but as the star of Shakespeare's theatre company, the Lord Chamberlain's Men, he was the natural choice for the part.

Richard Burton was directed by Sir John Guilgud in a 1964 stage production which used modern day dress and won Burton a Tony award.

Mel Gibson's performance in the Hollywood thriller *Lethal Weapon* is said to have secured him the role in the 1990 cinematic adaptation of *Hamlet*.

John Guilgud played the part more than 500 times over a 23-year period.

Ethan Hawke played Hamlet in an updated, film version of the play in 2000, using the Big Apple as a modern-day backdrop for the bloodthirsty tale of betrayal.

Shakespearean theatre actor **Sir Derek Jacobi** also took on the role in a 1980 television production. Kenneth Branagh cites Jacobi's 1977 theatrical performance as *Hamlet*'s Claudius, as 'the reason I got into acting'.

Ben Kingsley took on Hamlet in a 1975 theatre production in Stratford. He cites it as his favourite role.

Sir Ian McKellan played Hamlet in a 1972 BBC production of the play that shot many of the soliloquies in extreme close up, often with McKellan's mouth out of shot.

When **Sir Laurence Olivier** directed himself in the 1948 film version of *Hamlet*, he became the first person to direct themselves to a best actor Oscar.

Although **Nicol Williamson**'s performance of the great John Barrymore playing Hamlet, in the 1991 play *I Hate Hamlet,* received critical acclaim, the tyrant is also known for stabbing co-star Evan Handler in the leg during a stage fight.

STATESIDE SHAKESPEARE

The New York Shakespeare Festival was launched in 1954 by influential US theatre producer and director, Joseph Papp. He spent a good part of his life making sure that the Bard was a permanent fixture in Central Park by using his Broadway hits, such as *Chorus Line* (1975), to finance the Festival's open-air performances. But money wasn't the only link between the two venues; his musical versions of *The Two Gentlemen of Verona* (1971) and *Much Ado About Nothing* (1972) were both so successful they were given extended runs on Broadway.

Papp went on to launch a Shakespeare 'marathon' in 1987. His plan was to produce all 37 plays in six years using the best directors and actors of the time. But while Papp did not live to see his plan become a reality, the marathon inspired some pretty big names, including Kevin Kline, Al Pacino, Vanessa Redgrave, Morgan Freeman, Raul Julia, Martin Sheen, and Denzel Washington. It came to a close in 1997, with [*King*] *Henry VIII*, the marathon's last play, shown at the Delacorte Theater in Central Park.

WRITERS ON WILLIAM

What needs my Shakespeare for his honour'd bones,
The labour of an age in piled stones?
Or that his hallow'd relics should be hid
Under a star-pointing pyramid?
Dear son of Memory, great heir of Fame,
What need'st thou such weak witness of thy name?
Thou, in our wonder and astonishment,
Hast built thyself a life-long monument.
For whilst, to the shame of slow-endeavouring art,
Thy easy numbers flow; and that each heart
Hath, from the leaves of thy unvalued book,
Those Delphic lines with deep impression took;
Then thou, our fancy of itself bereaving,
Dost make us marble with too much conceiving;
And, so sepulchr'd, in such pomp dost lie,
That kings, for such a tomb should wish to die.

John Milton, *An Epitaph on the Admirable Dramatic Poet, W. Shakespeare*

QUOTE UNQUOTE

*Playing Shakespeare is so tiring. You never get
a chance to sit down unless you're a king.*
Josephine Hull, nineteenth-century US actress

SHAKESPEARE THE STONER?

In 2001, scientists at South Africa's Transvaal Museum announced that clay pipe fragments dug up from the area around Shakespeare's home, carried traces of hemp. Their study was provoked by a re-reading of the sonnets, which unearthed references to, 'compounds strange' and, 'invention in a noted weed'. But Professor Stanley Wells of the UK's Shakespeare Birthplace Trust, who provided the pipe fragments for analysis, rebuffed the findings, saying in the Bard's defence: 'There are about eight million cannabis takers in this country at the present time. Are they producing anything comparable to Shakespeare's sonnets, I ask myself? I doubt it.'

POETIC PUZZLERS

Which of these actors has never played King Lear?
James Earl Jones
David Garrick
Kenneth Branagh
F Murray Abraham
Answer on page 153.

THE LUVVY OF LUVVYS

Not many actors have been able to single-handedly turn tragedy *Romeo and Juliet* into a comedy, but between 1809 and 1815, Robert Coates did just that – and he wasn't even trying.

Originally from Antigua, Coates favoured a 'play-it-by-ear' method of acting, which often seemed to have little to do with the script at all. Colleagues and directors griped when he routinely forgot his lines, invented new scenes or lines of dialogue, and over-acted the crucial death scene, but Coates was oblivious.

His reputation as London's most appalling and melodramatic actor, drew in crowds from all over the country, including Prince Regent (the future King George IV). And at each performance the packed house would roar with laughter and hurl insults and vegetables when Coates was on stage.

Many theatre managers were so fearful of rioting that they refused to allow Coates to perform. He, however, loved the fame, fashioning flamboyant costumes for his performances (enough to earn him the nickname 'Diamond Coates') and loudly proclaiming his belief that his acting skills were improving the classics.

The novelty wore off in 1815 and he later died in near obscurity in a street accident in 1848.

1567	Mary Queen of Scots flees to England.
1577	Sir Francis Drake starts his voyage around the world.
1569	Mercator invents map projection. The Wright-Molyneux Map, based on Mercator's invention, is mentioned in *Twelfth Night*.
1585	Anglo-Spanish War breaks out after growing trade clashes and anti-Catholic moves in England.
1587	Mary Queen of Scots is executed.
1588	Spanish Armada is defeated.
1589	King Henry IV – the inspiration for *King Henry IV, Part One* and *King Henry IV, Part Two* – ascends the French throne.
c.1590	Shakespeare's contemporary, Marlowe, writes *Doctor Faustus*.
1592	Galileo Galilei builds a crude thermometer.
1592-93	Theatres are closed by the black plague. 'Searches' for the plague are mentioned in *Romeo and Juliet*.
1596	Sir John Harington invents a flush toilet for Elizabeth I.
1598	Boris Godunov becomes the Russian Tsar.
1603	King James VI of Scotland, for whom *Macbeth* was written, becomes King James I of England after Queen Elizabeth I dies, aged 70.
1604	England and Spain make peace in the Anglo-Spanish War.
1605	The gunpowder plot is foiled. Allusions to the plot are thought to have been made in *Macbeth*.
1605-15	Cervantes writes *Don Quixote*, which inspired the lead character in Shakespeare's 'missing play' *Cardenio*.
1606	Ben Jonson writes *Volpone*.
1608	Hans Lippershey designs the first practical telescope.
1609	Kepler devises his laws of planetary motion.
1610	Louis XIII becomes King of France.
1611	The King James version of the *Bible* is published in England.

QUOTE UNQUOTE

Frankly Lear is an easy part, one of the easiest parts in Shakespeare apart from Coriolanus. We can all play it. It is simply bang straight forward. Not like Romeo for instance, where you spend the whole evening searching for sympathy. But then anyone who lets an erection rule his life doesn't deserve much sympathy does he?
Sir Laurence Olivier, English actor

NOT QUITE A RAVE REVIEW

English actor, Sir Herbert Beerbohm Tree (1853-1917) was highly praised for his performances of *Falstaff* at the end of the nineteenth century. However, the reception when he turned his attention to *Hamlet* was not as warm. 'They are going to dig up Shakespeare and dig up Bacon', said contemporary WS Gilbert (of Gilbert and Sullivan fame). 'They are going to set their coffins side by side, and they are going to get [Tree] to recite *Hamlet* to them. The one who turns in his coffin will be the author of the play.'

A LENGTHY YARN

The Bard certainly liked to give his actors and audiences a challenge...

	Play	Lines
1.	*Hamlet*	3,901
2.	*King Richard III*	3,886
3.	*Coriolanus*	3,820
4.	*Cymbeline*	3,813
5.	*Othello*	3,672
6.	*Antony and Cleopatra*	3,630
7.	*Troilus and Cressida*	3,576
8.	*King Henry VIII*	3,450
9.	*King Henry V*	3,368
10.	*The Winter's Tale*	3,354

At 1,782 lines *The Comedy of Errors* is Shakespeare's shortest play. The average length of a Shakespearean play is 2,832 lines.

SONNET SECRETS

Sonnets to a rival poet

Shakespeare addresses nine sonnets to a 'rival poet' who seems to represent a clear threat to his patron's ongoing financial support. In 'Whilst I alone did call upon thy aid' (Sonnet 79), he goes as far as to implore his patron to recognise his rival as a thief, and becomes increasingly desperate as his rival's prominence grows: 'But now my gracious numbers are decay'd,/ And my sick Muse doth give another place./ I grant (sweet love) thy lovely argument/ Deserves the travail of a worthier pen;/ Yet what of thee, thy poet doth invent/ He robs thee of, and pays it thee again.'

Most believe this threatening figure to be the heralded playwright Christopher Marlowe, whose death also coincides with the last of Shakespeare's nine sonnets to the rival poet.

Not every reader has appreciated the genius of Shakespeare, as these cutting comments go to show...

[Shakespeare was] crude, immoral, vulgar and senseless.
Leo Tolstoy, Russian author. Tolstoy's disapproval wasn't reserved simply for Shakespeare; in his critical study *What is art?*, he also had a pop at Beethoven and Dante.

Shakespeare – what trash are his works in the gross.
Edward Young, English poet

Hamlet is a coarse and barbarous play... One might think the work is a product of a drunken savages' imagination.
Voltaire, French philosopher. Although Voltaire rebuked Shakespeare for his use of language, poetic rhythm and coarse, everyday imagery (quite the torment for his refined French ears), he must have admired his tragedies for they had a profound influence on his own.

[Shakespeare] has played an unforgivable part in the debasement of elves.
JRR Tolkien, author of *Lord of the Rings*, and elf expert commenting on the 'unfair' depiction of elven folk in *A Midsummer-Night's Dream*.

The sonnets are hot and pothery, there is much condensation, little delicacy, like raspberry jam without the cream, without the crust, without bread.
Walter Savage Landor, poet

[Shakespeare is] a sycophant, a flatterer, a breaker of marriage vows, a whining and inconsistent person.
Elizabeth Forsyth, English writer

I have tried lately to read Shakespeare and found it so intolerably dull that it nauseated me.
Charles Darwin, expounder of evolution. Darwin was lamenting the atrophied part of his brain which, possibly through over-classification, could no longer find pleasure in 'higher aesthetic tastes', such as poetry and history plays.

I am more easily bored with Shakespeare and have suffered more ghastly evenings with Shakespeare than with any other dramatist I know.
Peter Brook, British theatrical producer and director

And Hamlet how boring, how boring to live with, So mean and self conscious, blowing and snoring. His wonderful speeches, full of other folks' whoring.
DH Lawrence, English writer, in *When I Read Shakepeare*

[Shakespeare's plays] are exactly the sort of plays I would expect a grocer to write.
Lord Byron, English writer and poet

QUOTE UNQUOTE

By the age of 15 Shakespeare had still taken no special hold of my imagination. I was interested in soccer and girls. Shakespeare was for swots. ...I think part of my interest began with having a bad experience with Shakespeare. I was made to read The Merchant of Venice *aloud in class. And it made no sense to me, it was like reading the telephone directory.*
Kenneth Branagh, arguably Britain's most famous living Shakespearean actor

OUT OF TIME

Period slip-ups only spotted by the fact-checking fan...

In *Cymbeline*, set during the reign of Augustus Caesar (27BC-AD 14), characters talk about 'France' and 'French women'. But France was known as 'Gaul' in Caesar's time, and would have been little more than a tribal wilderness.

In *Julius Caesar,* set just before the death of Caesar in 44BC, Brutus and Cassius hear a clock chiming in Act II, scene i. But mechanical clocks weren't invented until the fourteenth century AD.

Troilus and Cressida is set in the second year of the Trojan War (traditionally dated to 1260BC) making Hector's reference to Aristotle a little strange – the philosopher was not born until 384BC.

King Lear is well known for its ocular imagery, but Gloucester's declaration, 'I shall not need spectacles' (Act IV, scene i), is particularly apt: the play dramatises events from the eighth century BC, but glasses were not invented until the thirteenth century AD.

And one geographical error...
In *A Winter's Tale*, the Bard tacks a seacoast onto landlocked Bohemia. However, as his geographical sources were limited to early travel books and classicalepics we may let him off.

WRITERS ON WILLIAM

I remember the players have often mentioned it as an honour to Shakespeare that in his writing (whatsoever he penned) he never blotted out a line. My answer hath been 'Would he have blotted a thousand.' Which they thought a malevolent speech. I had not told posterity this, but for their ignorance, who chose that circumstance to commend their friend by wherein he most faulted; and to justify mine own candour: for I loved the man, and do honour his memory, on this side idolatry, as much as any.

Ben Jonson, *Discoveries*

TAH PAGH, TAH BE (TO BE OR NOT TO BE)

*'You have not experienced Shakespeare until you
have read him in the original Klingon.'*

So uttered Klingon Chancellor Gorkon in the 1991 film *Star Trek VI: The Undiscovered Country*. His call did not go unanswered. The US-based Klingon Shakespeare Restoration Project was promptly set up with a goal to restore all of Shakespeare's works into the 'original Klingon' – apparently the Bard's native language. It has so far painstakingly translated *Hamlet* and *Much Ado About Nothing*, and *The Complete Works of Shakespeare* are due to follow suit.

HOW DO WE KNOW HE ACTUALLY EXISTED?

The major items of documentary evidence that mention William Shakespeare include:

1. A baptismal record in the Stratford parish register on 26 April 1564.

2. A marriage bond and license issued for William and Anne in 1582.

3. A royal record in the treasurer of the Chamber about payment to Will Kempe, Shakespeare and Richard Burbage for two performances for Elizabeth I in 1595.

5. A property deed from 1597 for the purchase of New Place in Stratford-upon-Avon.

6. A 1598 listing of actors in Ben Jonson's *Every Man in his Humour*, in which Shakespeare is listed as a comedian.

7. A list from 1598 which records him as illegally holding on to 80 bushels of malt during a shortage.

8. A tax record from 1598 which lists him as a tax defaulter.

9. A letter written to Shakespeare in 1598, by Richard Quiney, requesting a loan of £30.

10. A mention by name in the lease for the Globe theatre in 1599.

11. A diary entry by John Manningham, a contemporary of Shakespeare's in London.

12. A list of actors in Ben Jonson's play *Sejanus*, where Shakespeare is mentioned as a principal tragedian in 1603.

13. A Master of the Wardrobe record from 1604 which lists Shakespeare as receiving scarlet cloth to be worn for the King's Royal Procession.

14. A property document from 1613, referring to the purchase of the Blackfriars Gatehouse.

15. His Last Will and Testament, filed on 25 March 1616.

16. The Stratford parish register note for his burial on 25 April 1616.

WHY DID SHAKESPEARE LEAVE HIS WIFE HIS SECOND BEST BED?

'Item I gyve unto my wief my second best bed with the furniture', commanded Shakespeare in his Last Will and Testament of 1616. But why the second best bed?

Much has been written about this odd bequest. But contrary to how it may appear, there is little reason to think it was a snub against his wife Anne (née Hathaway). The 'second best bed' was most likely the bed the couple used; the best bed was traditionally reserved for guests.

Some scholars even believe the bed was a Hathaway family heirloom, mentioned in the will of Anne's father and lent to the couple on the understanding it would eventually be returned as a Hathaway family possession.

But why just the bed and furniture? Under medieval common law, Anne Shakespeare would have already been entitled to one third of her late husband's estate. It was taken as read and rarely mentioned in the wills of the time.

RIGHT UP HIS STREET

Shakespeare Avenue, *Bath*
Shakespeare Close, *Liverpool*
Shakespeare Court, *Cardiff*
Shakespeare Crescent, *Castleford*
Shakespeare Drive, *Southampton*
Shakespeare Gardens, *Rugby*
Shakespeare Grove, *Wigan*
Shakespeare Lane, *Evesham*
Shakespeare Meadows, *Repton*
Shakespeare Passage, *Margate*
Shakespeare Path, *Swindon*
Shakespeare Road, *Plymouth*
Shakespeare Street, *Nottingham*
Shakespeare Terrace, *Sunderland*
Shakespeare Way, *Aylesbury*

AT HOME WITH SHAKESPEARE

Every year, Shakespeare's Birthplace in Stratford-upon-Avon draws throngs of visitors from around the world looking for an insight into the Bard's formative years. But the subject of whether he did actually live here is still open to question. Stratford's parish records offer some historical proof: John Shakespeare (William's father) was fined in 1529 for dumping a 'muck pile' outside his Henley Street home.

OLD PICTURE, NEW CAPTION

*With acting, writing and house management to think of,
a member of the Lord Chamberlain's Men wore many hats...*

POETIC PUZZLERS

Untangle these Shakespearean characters...

1. Cold Aire
2. Pie Halo
3. Palace Rot
4. Scour A Lion
5. Ripe Touch

Answers on page 153.

SHOWING HIS FACE

He's common currency

In 1970, Shakespeare appeared on the reverse of the British £20 note. The image reproduced the 1740 Westminster Abbey statue of the Bard and the balcony scene from *Romeo and Juliet*. They were replaced in 1992 by the physicist Michael Faraday and the Royal Institute Lectures.

QUOTE UNQUOTE

We're calling it Macbeth, Not Mackers, not The Scottish Play, none of the euphemisms. Macbeth, Macbeth, Macbeth – there, I've said it and haven't been struck down. There's supposed to be a curse on this play. Bollocks! The only curse is that it's so hard to do.
Gregory Doran, associate director of
the Royal Shakespeare Company

HOLLYWOOD HONOURS

Although there have been dozens of film adaptations of Shakespeare's plays over the years, not that many have won Academy accolades. The only 'straight' Shakespeare film to win anything is *Hamlet* (1948), Sir Laurence Olivier's oft considered 'definitive' adaptation of the play. Olivier himself picked up two Oscars, one for best actor in a leading role and one for best picture. The film also picked up best set decoration and best costume design.

Shakespeare in Love (1998) won seven Academy Awards. Best actress in a leading role went to Gwyneth Paltrow when she gave 'that' speech where she gushed on about love and life.

Best actress in a supporting role went to Dame Judi Dench as Elizabeth I, even though she was only on screen for seven minutes. The film also picked up best art direction/set decoration, best costume design, best original musical, best original screenplay and best picture.

The Academy also went a bit loopy about *West Side Story* (1961), which picked up nine awards. The adaptation of *Romeo and Juliet* picked up best supporting actor, best supporting actress, best art direction, best cinematography and costume design, best music, best sound, best director and best picture.

WRITERS ON WILLIAM

Some of Shakespeare's Plays, I have never read, whilst others I have gone over perhaps as frequently as any unprofessional reader. Among the latter are *Lear*, *Richard Third*, *Henry Eighth*, *Hamlet*, and especially *Macbeth*. I think none equals *Macbeth*. It is wonderful. Unlike you gentlemen of the profession, I think the soliloquy in *Hamlet* commencing 'O, my offence is rank,' surpasses that commencing 'To be or not to be.' But pardon this small attempt at criticism. I should like to hear you pronounce the opening speech of *Richard the Third*.

Abraham Lincoln, in a letter to the actor James Hackett in 1863

Some episodes of *Star Trek* that have taken Shakespeare as inspiration...

Episode: 'Menage a Troi' (Episode 72, *The Next Generation*)
Source: Numerous
Jean-Luc Picard quotes Shakespeare when assuming the role of Lwaxana Troi's jealous lover, including, 'Shall I compare thee to a summer's day?/ Thou art more lovely and more temperate' (Sonnet 18), and 'When I have plucked thy rose/ I cannot give it vital growth again/ It needs must wither' (*Othello*, Act V, scene ii).

Episode: 'How sharper than a serpent's tooth' (Episode 21, *Star Trek: The Animated Series*)
Source: *King Lear*
'How sharper than a serpent's tooth it is/ To have a thankless child!' (Act I, scene iv).

Episode: 'The Defector' (Episode 68, *The Next Generation*)
Source: *King Henry V*
Echoing the King, the android Data laments the isolation of power and the few merits possessed by kingship. His performance includes the line: 'I think the king is but a man, as I am' (Act, IV, scene i).

Episode: 'Sins of the Father' (Episode 65, *The Next Generation*)
Source: *The Merchant of Venice*
'Yes, truly; for, look you, the sins of the father are to be laid upon the children' (Act III, scene v).

Episode: 'Hide and Q' (Episode 11, *The Next Generation*)
Source: Numerous
The episode is dotted with references to Shakespeare's lines, including the misquote, 'All the galaxy's a stage', by the alien Q. Picard is quick to correct the error, quoting the actual line from *As You Like It* (Act II, scene vii) which begins: 'All the world's a stage'. To which Q responds: 'Oh, you know that one?'. The android Data also quotes from *Hamlet* when refusing the offer to be made human: 'Was is not one of the captain's favourite authors who says, "To thine ownself be true"?' (Act I, scene iii).

Episode: 'Encounter at Farpoint' (Episode 1, *The Next Generation*)
Source: *Henry IV, Part Two*
Jean-Luc Picard quotes 'The first thing we do, let's kill all the lawyers' (Act IV, scene ii) when discussing human life in the twenty-first century.

Episode: 'The Naked Now' (Episode 3, *The Next Generation*)
Source: *The Merchant of Venice*
The episode paraphrases a Shylock quote, originally used to emphasise the humanity of the Jews: 'If you prick us, do we not bleed? If you tickle us, do we not laugh? If you poison us, do we not die?' (Act III, scene i). The *Star Trek* version, voiced by the android, Data, appears as: 'When you prick me do I not... leak?'.

SHAKESPEARE IN SONG

Shakespeare's Sister, The Smiths
Romeo and Juliet, Dire Straits
Richard III, Supergrass
Brush up your Shakespeare, Cole Porter
Cleopatra's Cat, Spin Doctors
Macbeth, John Cole
Romeo had Juliette, Lou Reed
Anything by Shakespeare's Sister

FEMALE HAMLETS

Often considered Shakespeare's greatest part, the role of Hamlet is never taken lightly. But what's a Bard-loving actress to do when the best role is written for those of a male disposition? Why play it of course!

Judith Anderson (1897-1992)
Australian stage and film actress who realised a life long ambition to play Hamlet in a national tour of the US in 1973 when she was 71 years old.

Sarah Bernhardt (1844-1923)
French stage actress who became cinema's first Hamlet in the 1900 *Le Duel d'Hamlet*. She went on to star in eight motion pictures and two biographical films.

Kitty Clive (1711-1785)
British stage actress who took on the role while still a young actress in her twenties.

Charlotte Cushman (1816-1876)
American stage actress known for playing a variety of male roles including Romeo and Hamlet. She performed the full range in a farewell tour in 1861.

Julia Glover (1779-1850)
Irish stage actress best known for her comic roles.

Eva La Gallienne (1899-1991)
US actress and devotee of Sarah Bernhardt, she followed her idol into the role in a 1938 production in Massachusetts.

Siobhan McKenna (1923-1986)
Irish actress who played the part in a 1959 stage production.

Sarah Siddons (1755-1831)
Famous British stage actress who became the first-ever female Hamlet when she performed the role in 1775.

Diane Venora (1952-)
American actress who appeared as Hamlet in the 1982-83 season at the Public Theatre in New York. She is the only female performer to have taken on the role in the history of the New York Shakespeare Festival.

Asta Nielsen (1881-1972)
Danish actress who played Hamlet as a woman disguised as a man, in her own 1920 production of the play.

A ROYAL SEAL OF APPROVAL

King James I (reigned 1603-1625)

Born in 1566, the only son of Mary Queen of Scots, James reigned in Scotland as King James VI, before becoming King James I of the combined kingdoms after the death of Queen Elizabeth I in 1603. He was a great fan of the arts, and within 10 days of arriving in London, became patron of Shakespeare's acting troop, the Lord Chamberlain's Men, which thereafter became known as the King's Men.

It is generally thought that *Macbeth* was written as a thank you to the King, as it celebrates James's ancestor Malcolm and warns against challenging divinely appointed kings.

QUOTE UNQUOTE

No one can convince me that Shakespeare didn't make up words just to upset the actors.
Jack Lemmon, US actor on trying
to learn the part of Marcellus in *Hamlet*

DISGUSTING DISEASES

Never one to pass up a useful dramatic tool, no matter how unsavoury, Shakespeare frequently lent metaphorical purpose to a laundry list of bothersome blights. More often than not, that purpose involved one character giving another a particularly harsh tongue-lashing, giving rise to such memorable put-downs as, 'Thou art a boil, a plague sore, an unbossed carbuncle' (*King Lear*). The technique also came in handy when dramatis personae wished to dismiss an issue out of hand, as in, 'A pox on your [insert subject of grievance here].'

Shakespeare's strength of feeling on the topic increased the more intimate it became: syphilis, the symptoms of which include all-over rashes, genital lesions and corrupted facial tissue, was the bogeyman of his time, and he found occasion to curse the 'infinite malady', the 'hoar leprosy', and 'love's fire' – with 'How sweet and lovely dost thou make thy shame' (Sonnet 95), associating a 'canker' with 'lascivious sport'. Indeed, his imaginative fixation upon the illness – and the waning of his handwriting and output towards the end of his life – has led Dr John J Ross of the Division of Infectious Diseases at Caritas St Elizabeth's Medical Center in Boston to contend, in *Clinical Infectious Diseases*, that the Bard may have been a sufferer. A typical treatment for a patient of his day would have been to inhale fumes from mercury boiled upon a hot plate – a most debilitating regimen that Dr Ross argues would have done Will's writing speed no good at all.

SHOVE ME A GROAT

In *King Henry IV, Part Two,* Shakespeare refers to the game of 'shove groat' (a groat being the currency of the time), as played by Falstaff in the Boar's Head Tavern, Eastcheap. This ancient tavern game (known today – if at all – as Shove Ha'penny) is played with small disks shoved using an implement (or hand) to stop on, or within, a number of scoring areas on the board. It isn't the only game mentioned by Shakespeare – in *Antony and Cleopatra*, Charmian suggests to Cleopatra: 'Let it alone, let's to billiards.'

IN LOVE WITH SHAKESPEARE

Long before *Shakespeare in Love* brought the Bard and his life onto the silver screen and into the conscious of today's youth, generations of directors fell in love with the playwright's work. Laurence Olivier, Franco Zefferelli and Kenneth Branagh became figureheads of the trend, but Orson Welles was another well-known fan. Before his infamous *War of the Worlds* radio play of 1938, he endeavoured to popularise the Bard with broadcast versions of *Macbeth*, *Hamlet* and *Twelfth Night*. In later life he then went on to direct and produce film and theatre versions of Shakespeare including *Voodoo Macbeth*, set in nineteenth-century Haiti with an all black cast; *Othello,* which won the Palme d'Or at Cannes; and the ambitious *Chimes at Midnight,* which was based upon no less than five of the Bard's plays.

WRITERS ON WILLIAM

It is the distinction of genius that it is always inconceivable – once & ever a surprise. Shakespeare we cannot account for, no history, no 'life & times' solves the insoluble problem. I cannot slope things to him so as to make him less steep & precipitous; so as to make him one of many, so as to know how I should write the same things. Goethe, I can see, wrote things which I might & should also write, were I a little more favored, a little cleverer man. He does not astonish. But Shakespeare, as Coleridge says, is as unlike his contemporaries as he is unlike us. His style is his own. And so is Genius ever total & not mechanically composable. It stands there a beautiful unapproachable whole like a pinetree or a strawberry – alive, perfect, yet inimitable; nor can we find where to lay the first stone, which given, we could build the arch.

Ralph Waldo Emerson,
Journal

SHIPWRECKED SHAKESPEARE

The Complete Works of Shakespeare make a weekly appearance on the BBC Radio 4's popular *Desert Island Discs*. Celebrity guests chat to Sue Lawley about the eight pieces of music and the one book they would chose to take with them to a desert island. But they can't choose the *Bible* or *The Complete Works of Shakespeare*, because it is taken as read that they already exist on the island.

Not only 'the most important work in the English language',

The Complete Works of Shakespeare also has the advantage of being fairly lengthy, which would be helpful in whiling away the hours on a desert island.

The programme was first broadcast on 29 January 1942 and has run ever since. Some of the shipwrecked celebrities to have enjoyed the company of Shakespeare's works on the island include Engelbert Humperdinck, Sir Ian McKellen, Princess Margaret, Noël Coward and Margaret Thatcher.

GHOSTS AND GHOULIES

Shakespeare's most emotive brushes with the supernatural:

The witches with cauldrons, spells and potions in *Macbeth*.

The ghost of Hamlet's father instructing him to avenge his murder in *Hamlet*

The fairies, spells, potions and mythical woodland in *A Midsummer-Night's Dream*

The ghosts of the 11 people murdered by Richard III in *Richard III*

Caesar's ghost, foretelling Marcus Brutus's downfall in the next day's battle in *Julius Caesar*

The monster, Caliban, the magician, Prospero, and the spirit Ariel in *The Tempest*

SHAKESPEARE'S DUST

When a graveyard became full in Shakespeare's time, existing corpses were often exhumed and relocated, so that others could be buried in their place. If Shakespeare did write his epitaph, as is commonly thought, he was evidently less than impressed at the practice; in fittingly poetic style he clearly requests his grave be left undisturbed:

> *Good friend for Jesus sake forbeare*
> *To digg the dust enclosed heare!*
> *Blest be the man that spares these stones*
> *And curst be he that moves my bones.'*

One of the best-known portraits of Shakespeare was uncovered as a fraud by experts at Britain's National Portrait Gallery in 2005. The image of Shakespeare wearing a wide white collar is often printed on the covers of his plays, but many scholars had long suspected that the work, known as 'The Flower Portrait' (above) was painted more recently than the 1609 date on the image. Analysis had uncovered chrome yellow paint from around 1814 embedded in the painting, dating the portrait to nearly 200 years after his death, a time when there was a marked resurgence of interest in Shakespeare's plays.

'M'S THE WORD

'The Unmentionable,' 'That Play,' and 'The Scottish Play' are alternatives to the title of *Macbeth* within the superstitious members of the acting profession. Anyone found uttering the 'M' word inside a dressing room has historically had to follow an elaborate ritual to escape the curse. This includes leaving the room, turning around three times, breaking wind, spitting, swearing, knocking on the door and asking permission to re-enter. The easier alternative is to recite 'Angels and ministers of grace defend us,' from *Hamlet* (Act I, scene iv).

Food makes a good showing in all of Shakespeare's plays...

Give them great meals of **beef** and iron and steel, they will eat like wolves and fight like devils.
Henry V, Act III, scene vii

...And, most dear actors, eat no **onions** nor **garlic**, for we are to utter sweet breath
A Midsummer-Night's Dream, Act IV, scene ii

Heavens defend me from that Welsh fairy, lest he transform me to a piece of **cheese**!
The Merry Wives of Windsor, Act V, scene v

Truly, thou art damned like an ill-roasted **egg**, all on one side.
As You Like It, Act III, scene ii

I fear it is too choleric a meat./ How say you to a fat **tripe** finely broil'd?
The Taming of the Shrew, Act IV, scene iii

Come, Kate, sit down; I know you have a stomach./ Will you give thanks, sweet Kate; or else shall I?/ What's this? **mutton**?
The Taming of the Shrew, Act IV, scene i

Come, shall we go and kill us **venison**?
As You Like It, Act II, scene i

My doe with the black scut! Let the sky rain **potatoes**
The Merry Wives of Windsor, Act V, scene v

How have you made division of yourself?/ An **apple**, cleft in two, is not more twin/ Than these two creatures. Which is Sebastian?
Twelfth Night, Act V, scene i

He tells me flatly, there is no mercy for me in heaven, because I am a Jew's daughter: and he says, you are no good member of the commonwealth, for in converting Jews to Christians, you raise the price of **pork**.
The Merchant of Venice, Act III, scene v

My Lord of Ely, when I was last in Holborn,/ I saw good **strawberries** in your garden there./ I do beseech you send for some of them.
Richard III, Act III, scene iv

Give it a **plum**, a **cherry**, and a **fig**./ There's a good grandam!
King John, Act II, scene i

Nay, you shall see my orchard, where, in an arbour, we will eat a lost year's **pippin** of mine own grafting, with a dish of **caraways**, and so forth.
Henry IV, Part Two, Act V, scene iii

You have made good work,/ You and your apron-men; you that stood so up much/ Upon the voice of occupation and/ The breath of **garlic**-eaters!
Coriolanus, Act IV, scene vi

RARE ROLES

The average number of roles in a Shakespeare play is 21. Shakespeare-an comedies tend to have fewer characters while histories have the most; leaving some comedic actors to argue that the less characters in a play the more precious the role. Here are the 10 plays with the fewest roles...

The Two Gentlemen of Verona – 13 players
Othello – 13 players
Coriolanus – 13 players
Twelfth Night – 13 players
The Taming of the Shrew – 14 players
King Lear – 14 players
Cymbeline – 14 players
All's Well That Ends Well – 14 players
The Tempest – 16 players
Much Ado About Nothing – 16 players

WRITERS ON WILLIAM

Only the best actors can pull off a convincing performance of Hamlet, as this fictional account by Pip, in Dickens's Great Expectations, *goes to show. Pip is retelling a less than successful performance by flamboyant family friend and wannabe actor, Mr Wopsle:*

Upon my unfortunate townsman incidents accumulated with playful effect. Whenever that undecided Prince had to ask a question or a state a doubt, the public helped him out with it. As for example; on the question whether 'twas nobler in the mind to suffer, some roared yes, and some no, and some inclining to both opinions said 'toss up for it;' and quite a Debating Society arose. When asked what should such fellows as he do crawling between earth and heaven, he was encouraged with loud cries of 'Hear, hear!' When he appeared with his stocking disordered (its disorder expressed, according to usage, by one very neat fold in the top, which I suppose to be always got up with a flat iron), a conversation took place in the gallery respecting the paleness of his leg, and whether it was occasioned by the turn the ghost had given him. On his taking the recorders – very like a little black flute that had just been played in the orchestra or handed out at the door – he was called upon unanimously for Rule Britannia. When he recommended the player not to saw the air thus, the sulky man said, 'And don't *you* do it, neither; you're a deal worse than him!' And I grieve to add that peals of laughter greeted Mr Wopsle on every one of these occasions.

Charles Dickens,
Great Expectations

Henry Wriothesley, Third Earl of Southampton

An influential member of Queen Elizabeth I's Court and a popular patron of poets, Henry Wriothesley (1573-1624) has been linked (in patronage) to poets such as Thomas Nashe, Gervase Markham, Barnabe Barnes and John Florio and, of course most famously, Shakespeare. It was to him that Shakespeare dedicated *Venus and Adonis* and *The Rape of Lucrece,* opening the latter with the lines 'The love I dedicate to your lordship is without end... What I have done is yours; what I have to do is yours; being part in all I have, devoted yours.' Although there is no evidence of a romantic attachment, there has been much speculation about their relationship, with Wriothesley often cited as the identity of the 'WH' flattered by Shakespeare in his first 17 sonnets.

Southampton fell out of favour with the Elizabethan Court in 1601, when he was implicated in an attempted coup, and sentenced to death, later reduced to life imprisonment. However King James I released and readmitted the Earl to the Royal Court when he ascended to the throne in 1603. Wriothesley's interest in theatre then took him onto the royal stage in a 1603 performance of *Love's Labour's Lost*. He died of a fever in Spain in 1624.

QUOTE UNQUOTE

Well, um, you know, something's neither good nor bad but thinking makes it so, I suppose, as Shakespeare said.
Donald Rumsfeld, US Defence Secretary, when asked why the US were unable to pinpoint the location of Osama Bin Laden

---

POETIC PUZZLERS

Name the play from its closing line...

1. 'To part the glories of this happy day.'
2. 'Well, while I live I'll fear no other thing so sore as keeping safe Nerissa's ring.'
3. 'Think not on him till tomorrow, I'll devise thee brave punishments for him. Strike up, pipers.'
4. 'One feast, one house, one mutual happiness.'
5. 'But I will rule both her, the King, and realm.'
6. 'The words of Mercury are harsh after the songs of Apollo. You that way: we this way.'
7. 'This heavy act with heavy heart relate.'
8. 'And now let's go hand in hand, not one before the other.'

Answers on page 153.

Total number of film and television adaptations of Hamlet *on publication* 41
of this book

NOT JUST A NAME

In choosing his characters' names, Shakespeare took delight in picking names that gave a clue to their personality...

Bottom *A Midsummer Night's Dream* – Not just a comic name for a comic role, the name also reflects the character's social status at the bottom of the social ladder. He is later given an ass's head.

Perdita *The Winters Tale* – Italian for 'lost one', the name reflects Perdita's abandonment as baby.

Imogen *Cymbeline* – Named 'the innocent one', Imogen's supposed infidelity to her husband sparks much of the action in the play. Ramming home the message, her alias is named **Fidele**, meaning 'the faithful one'.

Malvolio *Twelfth Night* – Italian for 'ill-will' (bad-feeling or unfriendliness), Shakespeare's audiences would have known from the start that this was an unsavoury character.

Marina *Pericles, Prince of Tyre* – Latin for 'belonging to the sea', this is a fitting name for a character born during a tempest.

Miranda *The Tempest* – Latin for 'the admired one', the name reflects the character's importance and standing. She is revered by her father and loved by Ferdinand.

A ROMANTIC SETTING

Every St Valentine's Day, the Italian city of Verona (the setting for Shakespeare's *Romeo and Juliet*) says it receives about 1,000 letters and cards addressed simply to 'Juliet'.

DON'T QUOTE ME

Singer Barbra Streisand mistakenly attributed a quote to Shakespeare during a fundraising concert for the US Democratic Party in 2002. She recited lines she believed to be from *Julius Caesar*, as she urged the party to oppose the Republican stance on Iraq: 'Beware the leader who bangs the drums of war in order to whip the citizenry into a patriotic fervour,' she said of George W Bush, 'for patriotism is indeed a double-edged sword. It both emboldens the blood, just as it narrows the mind. And when the drums of war have reached a fever pitch and the blood boils with hate and the mind has closed, the leader will have no need in seizing the rights of the citizenry. Rather, the citizenry, infused with fear and blinded with patriotism, will offer up all of their rights unto the leader, and gladly so. How do I know? For this is what I have done. And I am Caesar.' The quote was later attributed to an internet prankster. 'It doesn't detract from the fact that the words themselves are powerful and true, and beautifully written', Streisand said in her defence.

Edward III

Edward III works as a sequel to *Edward II* (by Christopher Marlowe) and as a prequel to *King Richard II* (by Shakespeare), causing much debate over its authorship. It was first attributed to Shakespeare in a 1595 bookseller's catalogue, but then rumoured to be the work of one or more anonymous actors or stage-hands. In the 1990s, however, Eric Sams put forward the idea that, although it was likely to be a collaborative effort, it was Shakespeare who took charge at a late stage of writing. He presented the argument in his 1996 *Shakespeare and Edward III*, but the idea was, at first, poorly received by academics. It was not until the results of US computer analysis of the play's vocabulary – including the repetition of the phrase 'Lilies that fester smell far worse than weeds,' from 'They that have power to hurt and will do none' (Sonnet 94) , that the question of Shakespeare's authorship was given legitimacy. To give authority to the claim, *The New Arden Shakespeare Series* included the play in its 1998 edition. However, it is yet to be included in any major Shakespeare editions.

QUOTE UNQUOTE

I'm pretty sure I can get through the killing of Desdemona eight times a week... but then, you see, I have another 25 minutes of stage time after she's dead. All Desdemona has to do at that point is lie in bed. There are stories of Desdemonas who have actually fallen asleep and come to with a great start, wondering where they were.
Patrick Stewart, English actor

A MAN OF ALL TRADES

B Shakespeare & Co Ltd – Scrap metal merchants, *Kingswinford*
JB Shakespeare Ltd – Funeral directors, *Croydon*
SB Shakespeare Ltd – Used car dealers, *Dudley*
Shakespeare's Landscapes – Landscape Gardeners, *Bognor Regis*
JT Shakespeare & Co Ltd – Carpet and rug retailers, *Stoke on Trent*
M Shakespeare – Painters and decorators, *High Wycombe*
Shakespeare Primary School, *Fleetwood*
Shakespeare's Store – Groceries, *Andover*
Shakespeare Motors – Garage services, *Southport*
Shakespeare's – Hairdressers, *Newcastle*
Shakespeare's – Estate Agents, *Solihull*
Shakespeare Driving School – Driving School, *Kidderminster*
Shakespeare Construction – Builders, *Birmingham*

When I read Shakespeare I am struck with wonder
that such trivial people should muse and thunder
in such lovely language.

Lear, the old buffer, you wonder his daughters
didn't treat him rougher,
the old chough, the old chuffer!

And Hamlet, how boring, how boring to live with,
so mean and self-conscious, blowing and snoring
his wonderful speeches, full of other folks' whoring!

And Macbeth and his Lady, who should have been choring,
such suburban ambition, so messily goring
old Duncan with daggers!

How boring, how small Shakespeare's people are!
Yet the language so lovely! like the dyes from gas-tar.

DH Lawrence, *When I Read Shakespeare*

WITHOUT THE NAUGHTY BITS

Working in the prim and proper Victorian age, Thomas Bowdler (1754-1825) is Britain's most famous expurgator of literature. He spearheaded the desire for decorum and modesty within plays and novels, and Shakespeare was not spared extensive attack from his red pen. Shakespeare's plays are 'stained with words and expressions of so indecent a nature that no parent would choose to submit them in uncorrected form to the eye or the ear of a daughter' he wrote, and with the help of his sister Harriet, proceeded to expunge all 'filth' and 'offensive behaviour' from the plays.

Readers of his *Family Edition of Shakespeare* (1818) were treated to a cleaned up version of the plays, where phrases such as 'your daughter and the Moor are now making the beast with two backs' (Iago to Brabantio in *Othello*) were replaced with such catchy alternatives as 'your daughter and the Moor are now together.' He also changed the death of Ophelia in *Hamlet* from probable suicide to a more palatable accidental drowning.

Bowdler believed his work was enhancing, rather than detracting from the original publications, claiming that Shakespeare had simply sexed-up his plays for the Elizabethan audiences of the day and that by removing the 'blemishes', he was giving further prominence to the 'beauties' of the work. And, while purists may have been horrified, Bowdler did manage to bring *Hamlet*, *Othello* and the rest of the plays, to a wider and younger audience.

HAMLET, THE ACTION HERO

Arnold Schwarzenegger, it seems, will turn his mind to anything. In the 1993 film, *Last Action Hero* we see his character, the time-travelling hero, Jack Slater, offer his unique interpretation on *Hamlet*. It is a somewhat speedier and less anguished dealing than in the original...

Hamlet [Slater]: Hey Claudius! You killed my father! Big mistake!

Narrator: Something is rotten in the state of Denmark, and Hamlet is taking out the trash.

Old Man: Stay thy hand, fair prince.

Hamlet: [Shooting him] Who said I'm fair?

Narrator: No one is going to tell this sweet prince good night.

Hamlet: To be or not to be?... Not to be.

THE LONG AND THE SHORT OF IT

Longest Scenes

Number of words	Play	Scene
7,137	*Love's Labour's Lost*	Act V, scene ii
6,856	*The Winter's Tale*	Act IV, scene iv
4,688	*Hamlet*	Act II, scene ii
4,677	*King John*	Act II, scene ii
4,198	*Timon of Athens*	Act IV, scene iii
4,278	*King Richard III*	Act IV, scene iv
4,216	*Measure for Measure*	Act V, scene i
4,402	*King Henry IV, Part One*	Act II, scene iv
4,076	*The Tempest*	Act I, scene ii
3,769	*Titus Andronicus*	Act I, scene i

Shortest Scenes

Number of words	Play	Scene
28	*Antony and Cleopatra*	Act III, scene ix
32	*Antony and Cleopatra*	Act III, scene viii
33	*The Merry Wives of Windsor*	Act V, scene iv
34	*Antony and Cleopatra*	Act IV, scene ii
44	*Coriolanus*	Act V, scene v
45	*Julius Caesar*	Act V, scene ii
46	*Othello*	Act III, scene ii
62	*Coriolanus*	Act I, scene vii
68	*Antony and Cleopatra*	Act IV, scene x
69	*Pericles, Prince of Tyre*	Act IV, scene v

Number of countries in which Professor Cass Foster's series of Shakespeare 45
abridgments, Sixty Minute Shakespeare, *can be purchased*

SONNET SECRETS

Sonnets to a young man

Shakespeare addressed his first 17 sonnets to 'WH', a young man of exceptional beauty, a fact that since has prompted much speculation about the poet's sexuality. Coleridge fretted in 1803 that the sonnets weren't entirely 'chaste', while generations of scholars have unveiled homoerotic references in his poems and plays, mostly revolving around the notorious pun on 'prick' in Sonnet 20 ('A woman's face, with nature's own hand painted'). However, in Elizabethan England it was not uncommon for a poet to express (or be commissioned to express) admiration and affection for a male friend through poetry. Indeed, these first sonnets weren't simply flattering, Shakespeare also urges his subject to marry – an unusual subject matter at the time.

Many believe the 'WH' in question to be the marriage-shy Henry Wriothesley, Earl of Southampton. Aged 17, Southampton paid a £5,000 fine rather than marry Lord Burghley's granddaughter, Elizabeth de Vere, making it more than possible that Shakespeare was commissioned to write the sonnets – one for every year of his life – to encourage him into marriage. Wriothesley did marry in 1598, but he never credited Shakespeare's verse for prompting him into the act.

POETIC PUZZLERS

Which of these actors has never played Iago?
Bob Hoskins
David Suchet
Laurence Olivier
Anthony Hopkins
Answer on page 153.

Answer on page 153.

THE SHOW WILL GO ON

Today Hamlet is a much-prized role, often saved for the biggest players. But this wasn't always the case. Stephen Pile, in *The Book of Heroic Failures*, describes a 1787 performance at Richmond Theatre by an inexperienced actor named Cubit – a novice who had previously only played small, walk on parts. Poor, untested Cubit became attacked by a *crise de neufs* after a poor reception on opening night and locked himself in the dressing room for the second performance, forcing the audience to sit through a production which omitted the character entirely. But it wasn't all bad. Sir Walter Scott reported that, not only was it an improvement on the first night, the audience also considered it an improvement on the whole play.

*The remarkable thing about Shakespeare is that he really is very good,
in spite of all the people who say he is very good.*
Robert Graves, English writer

WRITERS ON WILLIAM

'Did you say you bought back Shakespeare?'

'I did. I needed someone with a universal mind; someone who knew people well enough to be able to live with them centuries away from his own time. Shakespeare was the man. I've got his signature. As a memento, you know.'

'On you?' asked Robertson, eyes bugging [sic].

'Right here.' Welch fumbled in one vest pocket after another. 'Ah, here it is.'

A little piece of pasteboard was passed to the instructor. On one side it said: 'L. Klein & Sons, Wholesale Hardware.' On the other side, in straggly script, was written, 'Willm Shakesper.'

A wild surmise filled Robertson. 'What did he look like?'

'Not like his pictures. Bald and an ugly mustache. He spoke in a thick brogue. Of course, I did my best to please him with our times. I told him we thought highly of his plays and still put them on the boards. In fact, I said we thought they were the greatest pieces of literature in the English language, maybe in any language.'

'Good. Good,' said Robertson breathlessly.

'I said people had written volumes of commentaries on his plays. Naturally he wanted to see one and I got one for him from the library.'

...'I told the immortal bard that we even gave college courses in Shakespeare.'

'*I* give one.'

'I know. I enrolled him in your evening extension course. I never saw a man so eager to find out what posterity thought of him as poor Bill was. He worked hard at it.'

'You enrolled William Shakespeare in my course?' mumbled Robertson. Even as an alcoholic fantasy, the thought staggered him. And *was* it an alcoholic fantasy? He was beginning to recall a bald man with a queer way of talking....

'Not under his real name, of course,' said Dr Welch. 'Never mind what he went under. It was a mistake, that's all. A big mistake. Poor fellow.'

...'Why was it a mistake? What happened?'

'I had to send him back to 1600,' roared Welch indignantly. 'How much humiliation do you think a man can stand?'

'What humiliation are you talking about?'

Dr Welch tossed off the cocktail. 'Why, you poor simpleton, you *flunked* him.'

Isaac Asimov,
The Immortal Bard

'That which we call a rose by any other word would smell as sweet'
is one of the Bard's best-loved lines, but roses aren't the only flower
to appear in Shakespeare's plays...

Ophelia: And there is **pansies**,
that's for thoughts.
Hamlet, Act IV, scene v

Laertes: A **violet** in the youth
of primy nature./ Forward, not
permanent; sweet, not lasting;/
The perfume and suppliance
of a minute;/ No more.
Hamlet, Act I, scene iii

Ophelia: There's **rosemary**,
that's for remembrance; pray
you love, remember.
Hamlet, Act IV, scene v

Puck: The juice of [**pansy
blossom**], on sleeping eyelids
laid,/ Will make or man or
woman madly dote/ Upon the
next live creature that it sees.
A Midsummer-Night's Dream,
Act II, scene i

Gardener: Here did she
fall a tear; here in this place/
I'll set a bank of **rue**, sour
herb of grace:/ **Rue**, even
for ruth, here shortly shall
be seen,/ in the remembrance
of a weeping queen.
King Richard II, Act III,
scene iv

Duke Orsino: That strain
again! It had a dying fall:/ O, it
came o'er my ear like the sweet
sound,/ That breathes upon a
bank of **violets**;/ Stealing, and
giving odour!
Twelfth Night, Act I, scene i

Perdita: For you there's
rosemary and **rue**; these keep/
Seeming and savour all the
winter long./ Grace and
remembrance be to you both.
The Winter's Tale, Act IV,
scene iv

Arviragus: With fairest
flowers whilst summer last
and I live here, Fidele, I'll
sweeten thy sad grave. Thou
shalt not lack/ The flower
that's like thy face, pale
primrose, nor/ The azur'd
harebell, like thy veins; no
nor/ The leaf of **eglantine**,
whom not to slander,/
Outsweet'ned not thy breath.
Cymbeline, Act IV, scene ii

Ophelia: There's **rue** for you;
and here's some for me; we may
call it herb of grace o' Sundays.
O, you must wear your **rue** with
a difference.
Hamlet, Act IV, scene iv

Duchess: Who are the **violets**
now/ That strew the green lap
of the new come spring?
King Richard II,
Act V, scene ii

Titania: Come, sit thee down
upon this flow'ry bed,/ While
I thy amiable cheeks do coy,/
And stick **musk-roses** in thy
sleek smooth head.
A Midsummer-Night's Dream,
Act IV, scene i

48 *Year in the 1900s in which the film adaptation of* Hamlet *starring, and directed by, Sir Laurence Olivier, was released*

OLD PICTURE, NEW CAPTION

*Shakespeare's attempts to contain his thoughts at
night-time led to some interesting headgear.*

THE BOOZY BARD

William Shakespeare Pub, *Liverpool*
The Old Shakespeare Inn, *Sheffield*
Shakespeare's Head, *London*
The Shakespeare, *Scarborough*
Shakespeare's Joint, *Evesham*
Shakespeare Tavern, *London*
The Shakespeare's Head, *Brighton*
The Shakespeare, *Birmingham*
The Shakespear, *Hartlepool*
Ye Shakespeare, *Bristol*

A MIDSUMMER NIGHT'S JEAN

Levi's created a twist on *A Midsummer-Night's Dream* for their ad campaign in 2005. The modernised version of Shakespeare's epic fairy story – a scene between a jean-clad Bottom and Titania – takes place not in the woods, but on the streets of Los Angeles. The ad was well received, but for one slight slip-up: the two models are actually reciting the lines from the scene in which Puck gives Bottom the head of an ass, and Oberon puts Titania under a spell so that she will fall in love with the first 'vile' person she sees.

Position achieved by Shakespeare in Love *in the British Film Institute's list* 49
of the twentieth-century's top 100 films

In the morning Sir Archibald Flower, the mayor of Stratford, called at the hotel and conducted me over Shakespeare's cottage. I can by no means associate the Bard with it; that such a mind ever dwelt or had its beginnings there, seems incredible. It is easy to imagine a farmer's boy emigrating to London and becoming a successful actor and theatre-owner; but for him to have become the great poet and dramatist, and to have had such knowledge of foreign courts, cardinals, kings, is inconceivable to me. I am not concerned who wrote the works of Shakespeare, whether Bacon, Southampton or Richmond, but I can hardly think it was the Stratford boy. Whoever wrote them had an aristocratic attitude. His utter disregard for grammar could only have been the attitude of a princely, gifted mind. And after seeing the cottage and hearing the scant bits of local information concerning his desultory boyhood, his indifferent school record, his poaching and the country bumpkin point of view, I cannot believe he went through such a metamorphosis as to become the greatest of all poets. In the work of the greatest geniuses humble beginnings will reveal themselves somewhere – but one cannot trace the slightest sign of them in Shakespeare.

Charles Chaplin,
My Autobiography

DOUBLE TIME

In classical drama, plays followed the 'three unities' of place, time and action, as described by Aristotle. Each unity had its own set of specific rules: that the setting of the play should be in one location; that the action of the play should represent 'real time' (generally, the passage of no more than one day); and that all action should contribute in some way to the plot (no digressions or scene-padding allowed). Of all Shakespeare's plays, *Othello* follows these classical unities the closest. However, when it came to the play's time line, he did stretch the boundaries of credibility somewhat...

In less than a day and a half in *Othello*:

- Iago asks Emily 'a hundred times' to steal Desdemona's handkerchief.
- Rodrigo loses all his money, his land and his life.
- Cassio deserts Bianca for a week.
- Iago persuades Othello that Desdemona and Cassio committed 'the act of shame a thousand times'.
- Othello asks 'What sense had I of her stolen hours of lust?'.
- Lodovico sails all the way from Venice to Cyprus – a distance of 1,300 miles.

PROSE VERSUS VERSE

No play is free of verse, but five of the history plays are free of prose:

King Henry VI, Part One
King Henry VI, Part Three
King Richard III
King Richard II
King John

The choice between prose and verse usually comes down to class. Verse is usually reserved for nobles, whereas prose is employed for lower class or comical parts, such as Bottom in *A Midsummer-Night's Dream*. However, this is by no means uniformly true. For example, King Henry and Katherine in *King Henry V* speak to each other in prose, and Hamlet also speaks in prose in *Hamlet*. Lower-class characters also speak in verse, notably the Gardeners in *King Richard II*, Act IV, scene i.

QUOTE UNQUOTE

I did all the writing myself. I learned from a calligraphy person in the art department, and we studied his signature. Jesus! He must've gone through how many geese I would not know! You have to re-sharpen the quill after a page of writing, and if you're in the middle of a thought, you have to be deft with the knife.
Joseph Fiennes, English actor,
on playing the playwright in *Shakespeare in Love*

THE APOTHECARY'S WEIGHT IN THE PLAYS

Apothecaries were important medical practitioners in Shakespeare's age, and his plays demonstrate a sound working knowledge of various potions and tinctures, suggesting that the Bard had undertaken more than a handful of research visits. In *Othello*, Iago tells the Moor to forget about his peace of mind: 'Not poppy, nor mandragora,/ Nor all the drowsy syrups of the world,/ Shall ever medicine thee to that sweet sleep/ Which thou owedst yesterday' (Act III, scene iii). King Lear, on the other hand, begs for relief from a flight of rage using civet, a musky perfume obtained from a cat's scent glands: 'Give me an ounce of civet, good apothecary, to sweeten my imagination...' (Act IV, scene vi). However, Shakespeare's most famous chemical solution has to be in the instruction from Friar Laurence to Juliet: 'Take thou this vial, being then in bed,/ And this distilled liquor drink thou off;/ When presently through all thy veins shall run/ A cold and drowsy humour...' (*Romeo and Juliet*, Act IV, scene i). And we all know what trouble that led to.

QUOTE UNQUOTE

If we wish to know the force of human genius, we should read Shakespeare. If we wish to see the insignificance of human learning, we may study his commentators.
William Hazlitt, English writer

A DISAPPEARING ACT

Known as Shakespeare's 'lost years', there is absolutely no documentary evidence about the poet's life between 1585 (the baptism of his twins as registered in Stratford-upon-Avon's parish records) and 1592 (the first time he was mentioned in print as an actor in London).

Various theories seek to explain his activities during these seven years, including the most commonly-told story, as picked up by biographer Nicholas Rowe in his *Account of the Life* (1709), that holds that Shakespeare was expelled from Stratford-upon-Avon as punishment for deer-poaching. A second version was recounted by biographer, John Aubrey, in *Brief Lives* (1681). He proposes that Shakespeare was occupied as a schoolmaster during this time and cites as his source William Beeston, son of Christopher Beeston who had acted with Shakespeare in *Every Man in His Humour* in 1598. Aubrey argued that Shakespeare may have been inspired to write his first play, *The Comedy of Errors*, after teaching its source, Plautus' *The Menaechmi* in class, prompting him to join a travel-

ling theatre company passing through Stratford-upon-Avon.

In *Shakespeare: 'The Lost Years'* (1985), EAJ Honigmann offers a different interpretation of the schoolmaster theory. He believes Shakespeare's employers were the powerful Lancashire Hoghton family, arguing that their private theatrical performances (and contact with the Lord Strange's Men theatre company) could have led to Shakespeare's change of career.

Others have speculated that Shakespeare passed this time working as a conveyancer's clerk in the office of a prosperous lawyer, that he served as a military foot soldier in the low countries, that he was a scrivner, a gardener, a sailor, a printer, a money lender, a coachman, or that he simply went on an extended holiday to Italy. But, perhaps the most outrageous myth to have surfaced, is that 'Shakespeare' was actually an Italian named Michelangelo Crollalanza (Italian for 'shake spear'), who, aged 24, fled Italy due to his religious beliefs, settling in Stratford-upon-Avon under the identity 'William Shakespeare', before returning to Italy in quieter times.

SOME POETIC TERMS YOU HAD ALWAYS JUST PRETENDED TO UNDERSTAND...

Meter: an easily recognisable rhythm in verse, made up of a pattern of consistently recurring stressed/long and then unstressed/short syllables.

Foot: the basic unit of meter used to describe rhythm. A foot is made up of a number of syllables or stresses that form a line of verse. The structure and number of words are incidental, as feet focus on the stressed syllables and sounds. A foot can be several words, a single word or a combination of syllables from more than one word.

Iamb: a specific type of metric foot that consists of two syllables, an unstressed/short syllable followed by a stressed/long syllable ('da DUM'). It is the opposite of a troche.

Iambic pentameter: a meter that is made up of five feet, with iambs representing the dominant foot, as in 'To be/ commenced/ in strands/ afar/ remote (*King Henry IV Part I*, Act I, scene i). This is the most common verse type in English (and German) poetry and is heavily used by Shakespeare.

Troche: a specific type of metric foot that consists of two syllables only, a stressed/long syllable followed by an unstressed/short syllable ('DA dum'). It is the opposite of an iamb.

Trochaic rhythm: A trochaic rhythm has a pattern of stressed/unstressed syllable, as in 'Double, double, toil and trouble;/ Fire burn and cauldron bubble' (*Macbeth*, Act IV, scene i).

BACK FROM THE DEAD

Falstaff, Shakespeare's most bawdy, comic character, appears in *King Henry IV, Part One*, *King Henry IV, Part Two* and *The Merry Wives of Windsor*. He is also mentioned in *King Henry V*, although he does not make an appearance. Fond of a drink and traditionally rotund, he has been played, among others, by Robbie Coltrane, Orson Welles, Ralph Richardson and Leslie Phillips. A popular character with audiences for his mix of cowardice and cunning, legend has it that Queen Elizabeth I was such a fan that she instructed Shakespeare to write a play about Falstaff being in love, even though he had already been killed off in *King Henry V*. Shakespeare didn't disobey the royal command, producing *The Merry Wives of Windsor* in which Falstaff is lured into a complex comedy of romantic manners after being caught poaching – and admitting it.

WHICH CHARACTER HAS THE MOST LINES?

	Role	Play	Lines
1.	Hamlet	*Hamlet*	1,422
2.	Falstaff	*King Henry IV, Parts One* and *Two*	1,178
3.	Richard III	*King Richard III*	1,124
4.	Iago	*Othello*	1.097
5.	Henry V	*King Henry V*	1,025
6.	Othello	*Othello*	860
7.	Vincentio	*Measure for Measure*	820
8.	Coriolanus	*Coriolanus*	809
9.	Timon	*Timon of Athens*	795
10.	Antony	*Antony and Cleopatra*	766

Hamlet speaks 11,610 words – the most required of any Shakespearean character, in one play. However, in *The Complete Works of Shakespeare* his word-count is outpipped by Falstaff, who appears in three plays: *King Henry IV, Parts One* and *Two* and *The Merry Wives of Windsor*.

SHOWING HIS FACE

Credit where credit's due

If you look carefully at the security stamp on your credit card, you'll see a ghostly image of Shakespeare. This 'stereogram' (similar to a hologram, but containing a sequence of live film footage, rather than a single image) captures the Droeshout Engraving of Shakespeare between the words 'cheque guarantee'.

POETIC PUZZLERS

Name the play from these familiar and not-so-familiar opening lines...

1. 'If music be the food of love, play on.'
2. 'I thought the King had more affected the Duke of Albany than Cornwall.'
3. 'Two households, both alike in dignity, in fair Verona.'
4. 'Escalus!'
5. 'Old John of Gaunt, time-honoured Lancaster.'
6. 'I learn in this letter that Don Pedro of Arragon comes this night to Messina.'
7. 'Boatswain!'
8. 'Before we proceed any further, hear me speak.'

Answers on page 153.

Baldrick: My uncle Baldrick was in a play once.
Blackadder: Really?
Baldrick: Yeah, it was called *Macbeth*.
Blackadder: And what did he play?
Baldrick: Second codpiece... Macbeth wore him in the fight scenes.
Blackadder: So he was a stunt codpiece. Did he have a large part?
Baldrick: Depends who's playing Macbeth.

Ben Elton and Richard Curtis, *Blackadder The Third*

A SHAKESPEARE CONNECTION?

At least one of Shakespeare's relations followed in the Bard's foot-steps – his nephew William Hart. The son of Shakespeare's younger sister Joan, William followed his uncle into the acting company, the King's Men, in the 1630s. However, the family tree doesn't end there. Even though William never married, he is rumoured to have illegitimately fathered the celebrated Restoration actor, Charles Hart, himself a member of the King's Men in the late 1600s. However, the coincidence of his name apart, no other link between the two actors has yet been proved.

SHAKESPEARE AND ESPERANTO

Seventeen of Shakespeare's plays, and all of his sonnets, have been translated into Esperanto, beginning with 'Hamleto' in 1894. The translation has been so successful that Esperanto advocates even go so far as to say that 'a Shakespearean tradition' exists in Esperan-to, spanning from 1910 when *As You Like It* was performed in Washington to the most recent production, *King Lear*, in 2001 in Hanoi, Vietnam. But do the translations reflect the majesty of Shakespeare's original versions? The Esperanto version of '*To be or not to be*' reads:

> '*Æu esti a˘ ne esti, -tiel staras*
> *Nun la demando: æu pli noble estas*
> *Elporti æiujn*
> *De la kolera sorto, a˘ sin armi*
> *Kontra˘ la tuta maro da mizeroj*
> *Kaj per la kontra˘staro ilin fini?*
> *Formorti -dormi kaj neniu plu!*'

Not everyone is convinced: 'It looks like some sort of wind-up-toy Czech/Italian pidgin,' said Justin B Rye on his website *Learn Not To Speak Esperanto* (www.xibalba.demon.co.uk/jbr/ranto/).

Even in Shakespeare's time, actors were plain big-headed.

A NEAT TURN OF PHRASE

William Shakespeare anagrams into:
I am a weakish speller
I'll make a wise phrase
He's like a lamp, I swear
Alas! I'm shrew-like ape
Wise male: ah, I sparkle!
A wee phrase? I am skill!
I sleep-walk a ham sire
We all make his praise
Here was I like a psalm

'To be or not to be: that is the question. Whether 'tis nobler
in the mind to suffer the slings and arrows of outrageous fortune.'
Becomes:
'In one of the Bard's best-thought-of tragedies, our insistent hero,
Hamlet, queries on two fronts about how life turns rotten.'

56 *Number of the sonnet quoted by Michael in the film* 10 Things I Hate
About You

Sir Thomas More

Four 'hands' (Hand A, B, C and D) are said to have contributed to *Sir Thomas More*, a dramatisation of the life of Sir Thomas More, the advisor who strongly opposed King Henry VIII's divorce from Catherine of Aragon. And since the 1870s, Shakespeare scholars have suspected that 'Hand D' is none other than that of Shakespeare.

A Pollard's 1923 *Shakespeare's Hand in the Play of Sir Thomas*, substantiates this claim through analysis of handwriting, spelling, vocabulary and imagery used. But anti-Stratfordians counteracted the claim by arguing that Pollard manufactured the evidence at a time when their claims that Shakespeare authored none of his plays were at their strongest.

SECRET OF THE PSALM

The King James version of the *Bible* was commissioned for the benefit of the Church of England under King James I of England. It was first published in 1611, and has had a profound impact on most of the English translations that have followed. But, what has this to do with Shakespeare?

A curious question has arisen over Psalm 46 in the translation, with many scholars arguing that it was in fact the work of Shakespeare. However, no documentary evidence exists to link the poet with the translation, and he is conspiciously absent from the list of translators assembled by John Bois and Dr Anthony Downes, the translators assigned to manage the project.

So why do people believe he was involved? Well, the forty-sixth word from the start is 'shake' and the forty-sixth word from the end is 'spear'. A coincidence, or Shakespeare's 'signature' in the translation? He was also 46 at the time it was published.

As satisfying as the coincidences are, there is much evidence to suggest it was just that – a coincidence. For example the counting of 46 words from the end of the psalm does not work if you count the word 'sellah'. 'Sellah' was used as punctuation and is dotted throughout the translation.

Many sceptics have also drawn on previous translations of the *Bible* that already included the use of the word 'shake' and 'spear'. The *Geneva Bible* of 1557 and the *Great Bible* of 1539-40 both use the words in Psalm 46, and were both published before Shakespeare was even born. On top of this, 'shake' and 'spear' are not uncommon words in the King James version of the *Bible,* and the translation from the original is not inaccurate.

So, despite any likelihood that a fan of word-play like Shakespeare would pop his name into the psalm, it seems overwhelmingly unlikely that he actually did. But it makes an interesting conspiracy theory anyway.

NAMES INVENTED BY SHAKESPEARE

Shakespeare didn't only invent new words, he also created some new female names...

Jessica first appeared in *The Merchant of Venice*. It is thought to be based on 'Iscah', a minor biblical character in Genesis.

Miranda, from *The Tempest*, is derived from 'mirandis', the Latin for 'admirable, wonderful'.

Olivia, first appeared in *Twelfth Night*. The name is thought to be based on the Latin word 'oliva' (olive) or the boy's name Oliver.

Perdita was created for *A Winter's Tale*. It comes from the Italian word for 'lost'.

Perdita apart, these names have gone from strength to strength in the UK. In a 2004 poll of the top UK baby names, Jessica had climbed to third place and Olivia came in seventh.

SETTING THE STAGE

The Rose

When the remains of the Rose theatre was discovered by archaeologists in 1989, the international press went wild. Built in 1587 by theatre manager Philip Henslowe, the Rose was London Bankside's first theatre, and the fifth theatre to be built in London, and its remains offer a unique insight into the heritage of the Elizabethan stage.

Successful runs of Marlowe's *Doctor Faustus*, Thomas Kyd's *Spanish Tragedy* and Shakespeare's *Henry VI, Part One* and *Titus Andronicus* brought punters from the other side of the Thames, and soon started a trend for theatres on the South Bank. The Swan theatre was the first to follow, in 1595, then the Globe moved to join it in c.1598. This soon overshadowed the Rose, however, and it closed in 1606, virtually disappearing from the map.

Its re-discovery in 1989, along with the theatre's surviving records, has allowed experts to piece together its original appearance. It is thought to have been polygonal in shape with space for 200 audience members. But the excavations didn't get off to a good start. The remains were covered up for conservation reasons shortly after their discovery in 1989, and it wasn't until over 10 years later that the theatre site was reopened to the public, thanks in part to a campaign figure-headed by famous actors such as Ralph Fiennes and Sir Laurence Olivier.

The remains are still undergoing restoration and reconstruction work to secure the site, but the exhibitions department of Shakespeare's Globe offer tours of the site with expert guides. Visit www.shakespearesglobe.com to find out more.

SHAKESPEARE'S CONTEMPORARIES

Christopher Marlowe

Christopher 'Kit' Marlowe (1564-1593) was one of the Elizabethan era's most noted poets and dramatists. He was educated at Cambridge, moving to London in 1587, where he became an actor and dramatist for the Lord Admiral's Company. Reputedly in trouble with the authorities for his religious beliefs, he was due to be tried under charges of atheism, when he was murdered, aged 29, in a bar brawl by a drinking companion in 1593. Many twentieth-century theories have questioned this account, however, arguing that he faked his death to avoid a trial, that he was murdered for being a government spy, and, even, that he faked his death to become a spy. His writing career only lasted six years, but he managed to produce such great works as *Doctor Faustus* (1589), *The Jew of Malta* (1589) and *Edward II* (1592). He is one of the leading figures in the Shakespeare authorship debate; the theory being that he 'became' Shakespeare after faking his own death.

STAR-CROSSED WILLIAM

Up in the asteroid belt between Mars and Jupiter lies the small asteroid, '2985 Shakespeare'. It was discovered and named by US astronomer Edward LG Bowell in 1983, and is just one of his 550 asteroid discoveries. Not just a brilliant astronomer, Bowell is also something of a fan of literature; '2985 Shakespeare' is found after '2984 Chaucer'.

WRITERS ON WILLIAM

This, part of a letter by playwright Robert Greene to his friends and fellow playwrights Marlowe, Lodge and Peele, was published in his 1592 pamphlet Groats-worth of Wit, *after his death. Said to be the first recorded mention of Shakespeare in London's theatrical society, the letter historically marks the end of Shakespeare's 'lost years'.*

Base-minded men, all three of you, if by my misery ye be not warned; for unto none of you like me, sought those burs to cleave; those puppets, I mean, that speake from our mouths, those anticks garnisht in our colours... There is an upstart Crow, beautiful in our feathers, that, with his tiger's heart wrapt in a players hide, supposes he is as well able to bombast out a blank verse as the best of you; and, being an absolute Johannes Factotum, is, in his own conceit, the only Shake-scene in the country. Oh, that I might entreat your rare wits to be employed in more profitable courses, and let these apes imitate your past excellence, and never more acquaint them with your admired inventions.

Robert Greene,
Groats-worth of Wit

The Complete Works of Shakespeare takes the reader on a global tour...

Ancient Greece	*Timon of Athens*
	Trolius and Cressida
	A Midsummer-Night's Dream
Ancient Britain	*King Lear*
	Cymbeline
Ancient Egypt	*Antony and Cleopatra*
Austria	*Measure for Measure*
Cyprus	*Othello*
Denmark	*Hamlet*
England	*Cymbeline*
	The Merry Wives of Windsor
	King Richard II
	King Richard III
England and France	*King Henry V*
	King Henry VI, Part One
	King Henry VI, Part Two
	King John
France and Italy	*All's Well That Ends Well*
Italy	*Cymbeline*
	The Merchant of Venice
	Much Ado About Nothing
	The Two Gentlemen of Verona
	Romeo and Juliet
Italy and England	*The Taming of the Shrew*
	Cymbeline
Scotland	*Macbeth*
Sicily	*The Winter's Tale*
Syria	*Pericles, Prince of Tyre*
Turkey	*The Comedy of Errors*
	('Ephesus' as it was then)
Wales	*Cymbeline*
	King Richard II

60 *Age of Sir Johnston Forbes-Robertson, when he played Hamlet in the 1913 film of the same name*

The poems of the great playwright...

A Lover's Complaint

A 329-line narrative exploring themes of betrayal and seduction, this poem was included with the first edition of Shakespeare's sonnets in 1609.

The Phoenix and the Turtle

An allegorical work depicting the love and death of two birds: the phoenix and the turtledove. This poem was first included in an anthology called *Love's Martyr*, assembled in 1601 by Robert Chester.

The Passionate Pilgrim

A collection of 25 poems first published in 1599 and attributed on the title-page to William Shakespeare. Only five of the poems in the collection can actually be identified as his work, however. These include 'When my love swears that she is made of truth' (Sonnet 138), 'Two loves I have of comfort and despair' (Sonnet 144), and three passages from *Love's Labour's Lost*. The remainder are poems by Christopher Marlowe, Walter Raleigh, and several unknown authors. *The Passionate Pilgrim* (1599) was published by William Jaggard who also published the First Folio in 1623.

The Rape of Lucrece

A narrative poem, drawn from Roman literature, which depicts the consequences of the rape of the Roman matron, Lucretia (Lucrece). It was printed in May of 1594, and appeared in several subsequent quarto editions.

Venus and Adonis

One of Shakespeare's longer poems, *Venus and Adonis* tells the story of two lovers taken from classical myth. Although now given less attention than his sonnets, it was a huge success after its first publication in 1593, and some even believe that the poem was the reason Shakespeare gained acceptance as a poet in London in the first place.

TOP OF THE CLASS

The annual Shakespeare Prize is awarded by the German Alfred Toepfer Foundation to British citizens who have made an 'outstanding contribution to European cultural heritage in English-speaking countries'. Originally established in 1935, the award includes a sizable prize sum of 20,000 euros and the chance to nominate a British student for the Shakespeare Scholarship, a year-long work and study placement in Germany. This prestigious award has had some rather distinguished past winners, including Iris Murdoch, Doris Lessing, Tom Stoppard, Sir Richard Attenborough, Simon Rattle, Graham Greene, Alec Guiness, Sir Derek Jacobi and Sam Mendes.

AN AGE OLD RIDDLE

How old is Hamlet? It's a question that has puzzled readers for generations. Some believe him to be 30 as in the play (Act V, scene i), the clown 'gravedigger' reports that he came to the churchyard in Elsinore 'the very day that young Hamlet was born'; and that, he has been 'sexton here, man and boy, thirty years'. But others dispute the gravedigger's words, arguing that Hamlet is still a university student, and one with an almost adolescent character at that. He doesn't appear young very often on the stage; only one of the major actors to have performed the role has been under 30:

John Guilgud	25
(at the first performance, 48 by the last)	
Nicol Williamson	31
Sir Ian McKellan	32
Mel Gibson	34
Kenneth Branagh	36
Henry Irving	36
Richard Burton	39
John Barrymore	40
Sir Laurence Olivier	41
Sir Derek Jacobi	42
Sarah Bernhardt	56

QUOTE UNQUOTE

Shakespeare was a dramatist of note,
who lived by writing things to quote.
HC Bunner, nineteenth-century US writer

REVEALING THE REVELS

The Master of the Revels was an officer of the royal household who controlled which plays made it onto the stage in Elizabethan times. The post was originally devised to make sure the Royal Court was able to see the best of the contemporary productions, but by 1606, the Master of Revels had taken charge of every play being performed, including their publication and censorship.

This increase in influence and power came under Edmund Tylney (1579-1610), the Master of the Revels, who was in charge during much of Shakespeare's theatrical career. He was the man to impress and fear, not only auditioning the acting troupes, but also editing their productions. If the Master saw fit, he would delete entire scenes from the playwrights' works.

The few known facts about Shakespeare's wife Anne (née Hathaway)...

• She is thought to have been the illiterate daughter of farmer Richard Hathaway, born in 1556 in Shotterly, a small village near Stratford-upon-Avon.

• The first mention of Anne's name is in the Stratford parish records, registering Shakespeare's intention to marry her.

• Six months after their marriage, Anne gave birth to their first child, giving rise to the popular theory that Shakespeare was forced into a hasty marriage.

• Anne was older than and out-lived William, a husband she did not see for great periods of their time together. On their marriage, she was 26; Shakespeare was only 18. After the marriage, Anne remained in Stratford-upon-Avon while William went to London to act and write.

• Anne gave birth to the couple's twins in 1585.

• She appears to have spent the remainder of her life in Strat-ford, outliving Shakespeare by seven years.

• On Anne's death in 1623, she was buried next to her husband.

Anne may also have inspired one of Shakespeare's earliest surviving sonnets (Sonnet 145)...

Those lips that Love's own hand did make
Breath'd forth the sound that said I hate
To me that languish'd for her sake:
But when she saw my woeful state,
Straight in her heart did mercy come.
Chiding that tongue, that ever sweet
Was used in giving gentle doom:
And taught it thus anew to greet:
'I hate' she alter'd with an end
That follow'd it as gentle day
Doth follow night, who like a fiend
From heaven to hell is flown away.
'I hate' from hate away she threw,
And sav'd my life, saying 'not you'

Certain scholars believe that Shakespeare was playing with the sounds of words in the final line to spell out Anne's name: 'Hate away' becom-ing Hathaway; 'And sav'd my life' transformed into 'Anne saved my life.' If so, that would discount the popular theory that Shakespeare was forced into a shot-gun wedding by Anne's pregnancy.

Number of the sonnet, opening with the line, 'Against my love shall be, as I 63 am now', in which Shakespeare rails against the ageing process

Oh no – Titus has made another pie...

QUOTE UNQUOTE

Shakespeare! You all remember Shakespeare. He wrote all them famous plays one after the other, then he went into a big slump and he ain't done anything good in years.
Robert De Niro, as Jake LaMotta, in *Raging Bull*

LOVE IN A HARSH CLIMATE

William Henry Ireland (1777-1835) claimed at the age of 19 to have discovered love letters from Shakespeare to his mistress, a new version of *King Lear*, part of *Hamlet* and two unknown Shakespeare plays entitled *Vortigern* and *King Henry II*, both handwritten. The experts of the day pronounced them genuine and *Vortigern* was produced at the Drury Lane Theatre in 1796. However, the audience knew better and hooted with derision at the final scene. Ireland eventually admitted that all the documents were forged.

POETIC PUZZLERS

Which of the following is the odd one out?

Syria

Italy

Navarre

Austria

Answer on page 153.

SHAKESPEARE THE FREEMASON

Is Shakespeare responsible for the funny handshakes, bizarre rituals and clandestine discussions that take place in strange temples inspired by the ancient Egyptians and early mystical Christians?

Were his plays and sonnets nothing less than the blueprint for modern freemasonry?

The answer to both those questions is yes, if certain scholars are to be believed. They are convinced that Shakespeare was the founding father of the notorious secret society, the Freemasons.

The First Folio of 1623 is considered to hold the proof of these deep connections. According to Alfred Dodd, author of *Shakespeare: Creator of Freemasonry*, the First Folio is packed with thinly veiled references to many aspects of freemasonry. He points to the regular appearance of words such as 'brother' (479 times), 'compass' (32 times), 'lodge' (24 times) and 'mason' (twice) as evidence of the Bard's knowledge of the Freemason way of life. Others have argued that the dedication in the First Folio is written not as if it were addressed to two noblemen (as it first appears to be), but to fellow Freemasons, suggesting that the whole thing, from blank page to final print, is an encoded message. One 'brother' has even claimed that *Macbeth* is an allegorical account of the murder of Harim Abiff, a core ancient figure in Masonic history who was murdered in the tenth century BC, in Jerusalem.

Proponents of the theory cite two events in eighteenth-century Masonic history as further evidence of their case. Firstly, it was on the centenary of Shakespeare's death, in 1716, that the Lodges of London met for the first time under a Grand Master to set up a Grand Lodge. Secondly, the Freemason's *Book of Constitutions* was published in 1723, exactly 100 years after the printing of the First Folio.

Could this be a simple coincidence? Freemasons north of Hadrian's Wall certainly have something to say on the subject. They believe their founder, William Shaw, was appointed by King James VI to re-organise the Masonic craft in Scotland in 1583, meaning that they were rolling up their kilts at least 100 years before the English were doing the same thing with their trousers.

Number of the sonnet in which Shakespeare proclaims that his 'love may 65 *still shine bright', if it lives on in the 'black ink' of his verse*

THE BIRTHDAY BOY

Every year on the Saturday nearest to 23 April, Shakespeare's fans gather in Stratford-upon-Avon to celebrate his birthday. Typically, there are several days of events including special performances of Shakespeare's plays at the Royal Shakespeare Theatre. The celebration starts with a Shakespeare Birthday Parade to Holy Trinity Church where Shakespeare is buried, and culminates with a Shakespeare Marathon around the town.

Stratford has been celebrating the Bard's birthday since 1769, but it was in 1824 that a procession through the streets to Holy Trinity Church was first arranged. Charles Edward Flower, the Chairman of the Shakespeare Memorial Association, who went on to establish the Shakespeare Memorial Theatre, extended the celebrations in 1864, by organising three weeks of celebrations around the anniversary, including performances of Shakespeare plays in a wooden tent next to the River Avon. The marathon was added much later, in 1982.

POETIC PUZZLERS

Name the plays from their last lines...

1. 'High order in this great solemnity.'
2. 'And Robin shall restore amends.'
3. 'Let our drums strike.'
4. 'What's yet behind that's meet you all should know.'
5. 'Go, bid the soldiers shoot.'
6. 'If England to itself do rest but true.'
7. 'We were dissever'd. Hastily lead away.'

Answers on page 153.

WRITERS ON WILLIAM

One other incident of the run of *King Lear* is, I think, worthy of record, inasmuch as it bears on the character and feeling of that great Englishman, Mr Gladstone. In the second week of the run he came to see the play, occupying his usual seat on the stage on the O.P. [Opposite Prompt] corner. He seemed most interested in all that went on, but not entirely happy. At the end, after many compliments to Mr Irving and Miss Terry, he commented on the unpatriotic conduct of taking aid from the French – from any foreigner – under any circumstances whatever of domestic stress.

Bram Stoker, *Personal Reminiscences of Henry Irving*, drawing parallels between the disposition of Gladstone and Lear's predicament in the play

66 *Year, in the twentieth century, when Ian Holm appeared as Prince Henry, and King Henry V in* King Henry IV, Part One *and* Part Two, *and* King Henry V

*Sex and violence is not that new. I mean, Shakespeare was
an actor too. So he wrote, it seems to me, things that he
knew actors would love to play.*
Laurence Fishburne, US actor

THE FIFTH GREAT BRITON

When the BBC launched a 'Great Britons' poll in 2002 to see who the
public would choose as their greatest Briton of all time, it came as no
surprise to find that Shakespeare was ranked in the top 10. But could
he beat the likes of Churchill and Darwin?

The final result was:

Sir Winston Churchill – 456,498 votes (28.1%)
Isambard Kingdom Brunel – 398,526 votes (24.6%)
Diana, Princess of Wales – 225,584 votes (13.9%)
Charles Darwin – 112,496 votes (6.9%)
William Shakespeare – 109,919 votes (6.8%)
Isaac Newton – 84,628 votes (5.2%)
Queen Elizabeth I – 71,928 votes (4.4%)
John Lennon – 68,445 votes (4.2%)
Horatio Nelson – 49,171 votes (3%)
Oliver Cromwell – 45,053 votes (2.8%)

The result may have been somewhat of a surprise. The Bard had been
voted 'British Man of the Millennium' by listeners of BBC Radio 4's
Today programme, beating all of the Great Britons in the process.

1. William Shakespeare – 11,717 votes
2. Sir Winston Churchill – 10,957 votes
3. William Caxton – 7,109 votes
4. Charles Darwin – 6,337 votes
5. Isaac Newton – 4,664 votes
6. Oliver Cromwell – 4,653 votes.

AT HOME WITH SHAKESPEARE

Shakespeare's home in Stratford-upon-Avon draws two million tourists
every year, hoping to learn a bit more about the playwright or to catch
a performance in the Royal Shakespeare Theatre (previously the Shakespeare Memorial Theatre). But the town was around a long time before
Shakespeare. The town has Anglo-Saxon origins, and developed as a
market town in medieval times. Stratford literally means 'ford in a street'
and indicates that the town provided a crossing on the River Avon.

SETTING THE SCENE

Acts with just one scene:

The Comedy of Errors, Act V
King John, Act I and Act III
Love's Labour's Lost, Act II and Act III
Measure for Measure, Act V
The Merchant of Venice, Act V
A Midsummer-Night's Dream, Act V
King Richard II, Act IV
The Taming of the Shrew, Act II
The Tempest, Act IV and Act V
Titus Andronicus, Act I
Twelfth Night, Act V

Acts with the most scenes:

Antony and Cleopatra, Act IV, 15 scenes
Antony and Cleopatra, Act III, 13 scenes
Coriolanus, Act I, 10 scenes
King Henry VI, Part Two, Act IV, 10 scenes
Troilus and Cressida, Act V, 10 scenes

QUOTE UNQUOTE

Entirely incidentally, a little-known fact about Shakespeare is that his father moved to Stratford-upon-Avon from a nearby village shortly before his son's birth. Had he not done so, the Bard of Avon would instead be known as the rather less ringing Bard of Snitterfield.
Bill Bryson, US author

SOME VARIATIONS ON THE NORM

Spellings were more freely phonetic in Shakespeare's time, and although now commonly spelled as 'Shakespeare', more than 25 recorded spellings were documented during his lifetime. They are:

Schaksp. • Shackespeare • Shackespeare
Shackper • Shackspere • Shagspere
Shakespe • Shakespear • Shakespeare
Shake-speare • Shakespere • Shakespheare
Shakp • Shakspe- • Shakspea • Shakspear
Shakspeare • Shak-speare • Shaksper
Shakspere • Shaxberd • Shaxpeare
Shaxper • Shaxpere • Shexpere

Year, in the 1900s, in which Sir Laurence Olivier's final contribution to Shakespearean cinema, a spoken prologue for Zeffirelli's Romeo and Juliet, *appeared*

Shakespeare has no direct descendants living today. He had three children and several grandchildren, but the direct line had died out by the end of the seventeenth century....

THE CHILDREN

Susanna

Susanna was Shakespeare's eldest child. She was born in May 1583, six months after William married Anne Hathaway. Susanna didn't have an education, and was never able to read and write. On 5 June 1607, she married a well-respected physician, John Hall, who had founded a prosperous medical practice in Stratford-upon-Avon. The match pleased her father enough for the couple to be appointed executors of Shakespeare's will. The couple produced just one child; a baby girl named Elizabeth, born eight months after the wedding took place. After her father's death, Susanna and John inherited and moved into New Place, Shakespeare's Stratford home. Susanna died in 1649, aged 66, and was buried next to her mother and father in the chancel of Holy Trinity Church in Stratford.

Hamnet

Hamnet was Shakespeare's only son, born in 1585, died at the age of 11 and was buried in Stratford Parish Church on August 11, 1596. Little is known about the life of the Bard's only son, but it is thought that he was named after Shakespeare's baker friend Hamnet Sadler. Even though it was customary for a boy from his background to be educated, there are no records that he attended school. It has been suggested that the lines in *King John*, beginning 'Grief fills the room of my absent child', illustrate Shakespeare's grief at the death of his son.

Judith

Judith was Shakespeare's youngest daughter. She was baptised in Stratford Parish Church on 2 February 1585, alongside her twin brother Hamnet. At the age of 31, she married Thomas Quiney, a 27-year-old local wine dealer and tavern owner. At first the marriage was happy, but on 25 January 1616, Shakespeare redrafted his will following the scandalous news that Quiney had made another girl pregnant. To make matters worse, it soon came to light that Quiney had not received the special licence necessary for him to marry Judith during Lent, and on 12 March 1616, the couple were excommunicated. Three days later, Shakespeare modified his will to ensure that Judith would receive the sum of £300, inherited in her own name, and left the bulk of his fortune to his eldest daughter, Susanna. Judith and Thomas Quiney had three boys; Shakespeare, Richard and Thomas. Judith died in 1662, at the age of 77.

Shakespeare had four grandchildren in total; Elizabeth, Shakespeare, Richard and Thomas. But Elizabeth, born in 1608, was the only grandchild that Shakespeare knew, as his grandsons were born after his death. Although Elizabeth married twice, she never had any children. Her first husband Thomas Nashe, died in 1635, just six years after they married. She received the title Lady Elizabeth Bernard, after she married her second husband Sir John Bernard. Elizabeth died in 1670, at the age of 62.

None of Judith and Thomas Quiney's children survived to continue the Shakespeare line. The Bard's first grandson, Shakespeare, was born in November 1616, but died when he was just six months old. Richard, born in October 1617, was 21 years old when he died in January 1639. Thomas, the youngest of Shakespeare's grandchildren, was born in January 1619. He died at the age of 19 the same month as his brother Richard in January 1639. It is thought that they both died of the plague.

THE ILLEGITIMATE SON

Sir William Davenant, a successful playwright and poet born in February 1606, is rumoured to have been the illegitimate son of Shakespeare. While living and working in London, the Bard's frequent trips home to visit his wife and children in Stratford-upon-Avon took him through Oxford where he would often stay at the Crown Tavern. The proprietor, John Davenant, was an influential man who had once held the office of Mayor of Oxford, and was married to a woman called Jane Shepherd Davenant. When her son, William, was baptised on 3 March 1606, Shakespeare appeared as his godfather.

William Davenant grew into a successful literary career. Following the death of Ben Jonson in 1637, Davenant was named Poet Laureate in 1638 on the strength of his plays The Witts, The Temple of Love, Britannia Triumphans, Albovine, The Colonel and Luminalia, and Madagascar. In 1656, Davenant attempted to revive English drama, which had been banned under Cromwell, with The First Day's Entertainment (or Declamations and Musick), and went on to create the first public opera in England, The Siege of Rhodes Made a Representation by the Art of Prospective in Scenes.

Apparently, rumours of Davenant's parentage started when Samuel Butler remarked that he, 'writ with the very same spirit that Shakespeare did, and seemed content enough, to be called his son.' William Davenant never made any attempts to defuse rumours he was fathered by Shakespeare, but there is no definitive proof either way.

Davenant died in his house, at Lincoln's Inn Fields on 7 April 1668, and was buried in Poet's Corner in Westminster Abbey.

70 Width, in millimetres, of the film used for Kenneth Branagh's Hamlet. It's the first Shakespeare film to have been shot in 70mm film

SONNET SECRETS

Sonnets to a 'Dark Lady'

Shakespeare addressed 24 of his sonnets to an anonymous woman who has come to be known as the 'Dark Lady'. She first appears in 'In the old age black was not counted fair' (Sonnet 127); but it is the poet's description of her in 'My mistress' eyes are nothing like the sun' (Sonnet 130) that is the best known. Described as 'a woman color'd ill' with black eyes and coarse black hair, the question of her identity has been debated for centuries. The most popular theories links her to be Jane Davenant, (the possible mother of Shakespeare's illegitimate son); Penelope Rich, (a powerful courtesan and patroness of the arts); Mary Fitton, (a lady in waiting to Queen Elizabeth I); Lucy Morgan (a brothel owner and former maid to Queen Elizabeth I); and Emilia Lanier, (the mistress of Lord Hunsdon, patron of the arts). Speculation rages, but the mysterious lady's true identity remains just that – a mystery.

QUOTE UNQUOTE

In order to act Shakespeare, you have to be a complete human athlete – not just a footballer or a philosopher, but both. His plays are the most thorough workout an actor can have.
Patsy Rodenburg, dialect coach

A TIPSY TROUPE

Some Shakespearean characters who are more than fond of a drop or two of the hard stuff...

Falstaff – *King Henry IV, Part One* and *Part Two*, and *The Merry Wives of Windsor*. He is the drinking buddy of 'Prince Hal' and in the 'Henry plays' is known to mooch around in drinking taverns on the wrong side of town.

The Porter – *Macbeth*. Offering a bit of comic relief in an otherwise dark play, the porter at Macbeth's castle drunkenly opens the castle doors to Macduff and Lennox.

Launce – *The Two Gentlemen of Verona*. Proteus's servant, and master to a badly trained dog named Crab, who keeps him busy when he is not in an alehouse.

Sir Toby Belch – *Twelfth Night*. Sir Toby does not believe in restraint and spends the whole play indulging in food and drink.

Stephano and Trinculo – *The Tempest*. These two characters spend most of the play drunkenly staggering around the island, offering some light relief from the arguments brewing between the other characters.

Bottom couldn't decide whether he looked better with the ass's head or without...

WRITERS ON WILLIAM

Mrs Bellamy tells us that she had the following anecdote from Colley Cibber – as Mrs. Mountfort during the time her disorder was not outrageous, she was not placed under any rigorous confinement, but was suffered to walk about her house – one day in a lucid interval she asked what play was to be performed that evening? And was told it was to be *Hamlet* – whilst she was on the stage, she had acted Ophelia with great applause – the recollection struck her, and with all that cunning which is frequently allied to insanity, she found means to elude the care of her attendants and got to the theatre, where concealing herself till the scene when Ophelia was to make her appearance in her mad state, she pushed on the stage before the person who played the character that night, and exhibited a far more perfect representation of madness, than the utmost exertions of theatrical art could do – she was in truth Ophelia herself, to the amazement of the performers, as well as of the audience – nature having made this last effort, her vital powers failed her, and she died soon after.

John Genest, *Some Account of the English Stage from the Restoration in 1660 to 1830*

THE MACBETH SUPERSTITION

What cursed *Macbeth*?

Some believe that Shakespeare intentionally included a powerful black magic incantation in his script, which drew a witch's curse. Others attribute it to betrayal and murder, while another camp link the curse to practical reasons; only one scene of the whole play is set during daylight hours and there is a high level of sword fighting and conflict, which could lead to accidents. But, most put it down to classic thespian superstition.

The superstition took a strange turn in August 2001, when Kevin Carlyon, the high priest of the British coven of 'white witches' and psychic medium Eileen Webster were summoned to the Old Inverness Castle in the Scottish Highlands. They had been asked to raise the spirit of Macbeth to discover whether it was he who had cast the evil spells on the play, and they were charged with exorcising the curse using 'the elements of earth, air, wind and water'.

'We have reflected the curse', Kevin Carlyon told reporters from www.thisisnorthscotland.com, 'but it will only be when people start saying "*Macbeth*" and putting on productions of the play, that we will know we have been successful.'

QUOTE UNQUOTE

Like all great romantics, Shakespeare realised love was a lot more likely to end with a bunch of dead Danish people than with a kiss.
Dawson Leery, teen character of US
television programme *Dawson's Creek*

LEADING THE LADIES

In the 2004 film *Stage Beauty*, Billy Crudup plays Ned Kynaston, a seventeenth-century actor specialising in the great female roles of the time (then traditionally played by young boys). It's a career that brings him much fame – a fame, that abruptly comes to an end with the arrival of women on stage. Of the people he would have blamed for this change in fortune, Margaret Hughes would undoubtedly have been at the top of his list, for she was the first professional actress. Hughes first took to the stage on 8 December, 1660, when she played Desdemona opposite Nathaniel Burt in *Othello*. Well aware they were making history, the production began with the reading of a specially-added, celebratory prologue, which contained the lines, 'I saw the lady dressed/ The woman plays today: mistake me not;/ No man in gown, or page in petticoat...' This effectively issued the smooth-voiced men and adolescent boys who had been playing female parts up to then with a mass P-45.

[William Bensley] had to play Henry VI in 'Richard the Third.' After the monarch's death in the early part of the play, he had to appear for a moment or two as his own ghost, in the fifth act. The spirits were at that time exhibited *en buste* by a trap. Now our Henry was invited out to supper, and being anxious to get there early, and knowing that little more than his shoulders would be seen by the public, he retained his black velvet vest and bugles, but discarding the lower part of his stage costume, he drew on a jaunty pair of new, tight, nankeen pantaloons, to be as far dressed for his supper company as he could. When he stood on the trap, he cautioned the men who turned the crank not to raise him as high as usual, and of course they promised to obey. But a wicked low comedian was at hand, whose love of mischief prevailed over his judgement, and he suddenly applied himself with such goodwill to the winch, that he ran King Henry up right to a level with the stage; and moreover, gave his majesty such a jerk that he was forced to save himself from falling. The sight of the old Lancastrian monarch in a costume of two such different periods – mediaeval above, all nankeen and novelty below – was destructive of all decorum both before the stage and upon it. The audience emphatically 'split their sides,' and as for the tyrant in the tent, he sat bolt upright, and burst into such an insane roar that the real Richard could not have looked more frantically hysterical had the deceased Henry actually visited him in spirit.

Dr Doran, *Table Traits*

A GREAT LOVE STORY

Ten artistic responses to *Romeo and Juliet*...

Roméo et Juliette – Hector Berlioz (1839). A symphony.
The Reconciliation of the Montagues and Capulets over the Dead Bodies of Romeo and Juliet – Lord Frederic Leighton (1855). A painting.
Romeo et Juliette – Charles Gounod (1867). An opera.
Romeo and Juliet Fantasy Overture – Pyotr Ilyich Tchaikovsky (1881). An overture for orchestra.
A Village Romeo and Juliet – Frederick Delius (1897). An opera.
Romeo i Dzhuletta Ballet – Sergei Prokofiev (1935-6). A ballet.
Romeo and Juliet – Constant Lambert (1926). A ballet.
Romeo and Juliet – Dmitri Kabalevsky (1956). A concert suite from incidental music.
West Side Story – Leonard Bernstein (1957). A musical.
Romeo and Juliet – Nino Rota (1968) A film score for the Franco Zeffirelli adaptation.

74 *Year, in the 1900s, in which Sir Laurence Olivier appeared in Jonathan Miller's television production of* The Merchant of Venice

THE WRITER OF THE MILLENNIUM

Shakespeare tends to do quite well in polls of 'the greatest writers', so it was perhaps no surprise that he was voted the 'Writer of the Millennium' in an online BBC poll, in 1999. He polled six times as many votes as the number two, Jane Austen, and the number three, George Orwell, combined. The top 10 were...

1. William Shakespeare
2. Jane Austen
3. George Orwell
4. Charles Dickens
5. Iain Banks
6. JRR Tolkien
7. James Joyce
8. Fydor Dostoeyevsky
9. Miguel Cervantes
10. Mark Twain

SETTING THE STAGE

Blackfriars

The Blackfriars theatre was the name of two separate theatres which stood, at different periods, on the same spot on the North Bank of the Thames, on the site of a dissolved thirteenth-century monastery. The first Blackfriars theatre – so called because of the monks' black clothing – opened here around 1576, when the building was leased to Richard Farrant, manager of a children's company, called the Children of the Chapel. It closed in 1584.

The second Blackfriars theatre opened in 1596 in another part of the monastery compound. It had been purchased by James Burbage, father of actor Richard Burbage, and converted into a private indoor playhouse, again leased to children's companies. It wasn't until 1608, 11 years after Richard Burbage inherited the theatre, that adult actors began to perform here. It became the home of the King's Men (the acting company of both Burbage and Shakespeare) who passed their winters in performance here, while continuing to spend their summers at the uncovered Globe. As a private theatre, the Blackfriars differed from larger open-air theatres, such as the Globe, by catering predominantly to the wealthy and educated of London. This was reflected in ticket prices, which were about five times higher than general admission to the Globe. The King's Men performed here without interruption until it was forced to close in 1642 on the outbreak of the English Civil War. The playhouse fell into disrepair, and was demolished in August 1655. Its site is today commemorated by Playhouse Yard.

John Fletcher

John Fletcher (1579-1625) is considered the greatest Jacobean playwright after Shakespeare and Ben Jonson. A prolific writer, he is estimated to have written or co-written 42 plays. Scanty records mean it is almost impossible to put together a full list of his works – especially as only nine of his plays were published in his lifetime. However, this is no reflection on his success – in his day he was considered as popular as Shakespeare. He collaborated with many of the great playwrights of the time, mostly with Francis Beaumont but also with Shakespeare, and he succeeded Shakespeare's as chief dramatist for the King's Men after Shakespeare was no longer active in the theatre. He died of the plague and is buried in Southwark Cathedral.

Fletcher's works include:
Philaster (1608)
The Faithful Shepherdess (1610)
The Humorous Lieutenant (1619)
The Pilgrim (1621)
A Wife for a Month (1624)

WRITERS ON WILLIAM

'That play must be a favourite with you,' said he; 'you read as if you knew it well.'

'It will be a favourite, I believe, from this hour,' replied Crawford; 'but I do not think I have had a volume of Shakespeare in my hand before since I was fifteen. I once saw Henry the Eighth acted, or I have heard of it from somebody who did, I am not certain which. But Shakespeare one gets acquainted with without knowing how. It is a part of an Englishman's constitution. His thoughts and beauties are so spread abroad that one touches them everywhere; one is intimate with him by instinct. No man of any brain can open at a good part of one of his plays without falling into the flow of his meaning immediately.'

'No doubt one is familiar with Shakespeare in a degree,' said Edmund, 'from one's earliest years. His celebrated passages are quoted by everybody; they are in half the books we open, and we all talk Shakespeare, use his similes, and describe with his descriptions; but this is totally distinct from giving his sense as you gave it. To know him in bits and scraps is common enough; to know him pretty thoroughly is, perhaps, not uncommon; but to read him well aloud is no everyday talent.'

Jane Austen, *Mansfield Park*

Quote-lovers take heed, you may not be half as accurate as you think you are...

Commonly: 'Bubble bubble, toil and trouble'
Actually: 'Double double, toil and trouble'
Macbeth, Act IV, scene i

Commonly: 'Discretion is the better part of valour'
Actually: 'The better part of valour is discretion'
King Henry IV, Part One, Act V, scene iv

Commonly: 'We are stuff as dreams are made of'
Actually: 'We are stuff/ As dreams are made on'
The Tempest, Act IV, scene i

Commonly: 'Alas, poor Yorick. I knew him well'
Actually: 'Alas, poor Yorick. I knew him, Horatio – a fellow of infinite jest, of most excellent fancy'
Hamlet, Act V, scene i

Commonly: 'The rest is science'
Actually: 'The rest is silence'
Hamlet, Act V, scene ii

Commonly: 'Music has charms to soothe the savage beast', Shakespeare
Actually: 'Music has charms to soothe the savage breast', William Congreve
The quote is accurate, but it is normally attributed to the wrong playwright.

Commonly: 'To gild the lily'
Actually: 'To gild refined gold, to paint the lily'
King John, Act IV, scene ii

Commonly: Julius Caesar: 'Friends, Romans, countrymen, lend me your ears'
Actually: Mark Antony: 'Friends, Romans, countrymen, lend me your ears'
Julius Caesar, Act III, scene ii. *This quote is normally attributed to the wrong character.*

Commonly: 'Now is the winter of our discontent'
Actually: 'Now is the winter of our discontent/ Made glorious summer by the sun of York'
King Richard III, Act I, scene i. *The word order is accurate, but by losing the second part of the quotation, the original – and more positive meaning – has been lost.*

Commonly: 'Methinks the lady doth protest too much'
Actually: 'The lady doth protest too much, methinks'
Hamlet, Act III, scene ii

Commonly: 'All that glitters is not gold' (or 'All that glistens is not gold')
Actually: 'All that glisters is not gold'
The Merchant of Venice, Act II, scene vii

POETIC PUZZLERS

Which of these actresses has never played Lady Macbeth?
Lynn Redgrave
Dame Diana Rigg
Angela Bassett
Dame Helen Mirren
Answer on page 153.

THE ORIGIN OF THE SONNET

The term 'sonnet' is derived from Italian, meaning 'little sound' or 'little song'. It has its roots in the thirteenth-century lyric poetry of southern Italy, which inspired the poets Guittone d'Arezzo and Dante Alighieri (author of *The Divine Comedy*), both of whom wrote verses in a similar style. However, Francesco Petrarch (1304-1374) is widely credited with having introduced sonnets to the rest of Europe. Crowned Poet Laureate in Rome in 1341, Petrarch's sonnets brought him considerable fame. His collection of Italian verses, *Rime in vita e morta di Madonna Laura* (c.1327), translated into English as *Petrarch's Sonnets*, are said to have been inspired by his passion for an idealised beloved named 'Laura'.

Petrarchan Sonnets are usually broken into two parts: an octave (eight lines), with an 'abbaabba' rhyming scheme, followed by a sestet (six lines), most often rhyming 'cdecde'. The octave traditionally states a problem or asks a question; while the sestet resolves the problem or question.

The sonnet was first introduced to England by Sir Thomas Wyatt and Henry Howard, Earl of Surrey, who both wrote in the style in the early-sixteenth century. By the late 1500s it had become fashionable for English writers to compose sonnets following Petrarch's pattern, and Shakespeare also wrote in the style in his early days. He went on to compose his own form (now known as the Shakespearean Sonnet), using an 'abab-cdcd-efef-gg' rhyming scheme.

Most Elizabethan sonnets were written about the joys and sorrows of love, but Shakespeare did not stick with tradition, ignoring not only the rules of sonnet composition, but also those of subject matter. He was happy to make fun of love, to touch on political events and to speak directly about sex.

Shakespeare wrote 154 sonnets in his lifetime. Mostly ignored by his contemporaries, they had a brief renaissance in the eighteenth century when used as a model by the Romantic poets such as William Wordsworth. Today they have been translated into almost every world language, including Esperanto.

Thomas Kyd

Thomas Kyd (1558-1594) was a hugely popular playwright in Shakespeare's time, thanks in part to his success with *The Spanish Tragedy*, which initiated an important Elizabethan dramatic genre – the revenge tragedy. Kyd is widely believed to have written a play entitled *Hamlet* before 1589, named 'Ur-Hamlet' by nineteenth-century German scholars. And he is thought to be the author of an anonymous play written before 1594 called *King Leir* with the same plot as Shakespeare's *King Lear*, except with a happy ending. Kyd's own ending wasn't quite so happy; accused in 1593 of holding unorthodox religious and moral views, he was arrested and tortured. Although he escaped imprisonment by implicating his friend Christopher Marlowe, his reputation was ruined and he died in poverty the following year.

QUOTE UNQUOTE

I don't make much distinction between being a stand-up comic and acting Shakespeare – in fact, unless you're a good comedian, you're never going to be able to play Hamlet properly.
Sir Ian McKellen, English stage and screen actor

STRATFORD-UPON-AVON: TOWN OF CELEBS

If you asked anyone who the most famous person to come out of Stratford-upon-Avon was, they would no doubt nominate Shakespeare. But the Bard isn't the only celebrity to hail from the Warwickshire town. Famous local sons and daughters include:

Antony Worrall Thompson – ginger-bearded celebrity chef
Gordon Ramsey – angry celebrity chef
Kate O'Toole – actress daughter of Shakespearean actor, Peter
Michael Ball – West End musical star and granny favourite
Neil Codling and **Simon Gilbert** – members of mid-nineties indie band Suede

Stratford has also had some notorious political candidates over the years. **John Profumo** was MP for the town in 1950, but hit the headlines in 1963 in a political scandal which linked him with a showgirl who was also involved with an attaché at the Soviet Embassy. **Screaming Lord Sutch** started his political campaign by standing as the National Teenage Party candidate, in the 1963 Stratford by-election that followed the Profumo scandal and resignation.

Identity Parade: the Droeshout Engraving (above left) and the Chandos Portrait (above right)

The most recognisable picture of the Bard is the portrait that first appeared on the front of his First Folio, seven years after his death. Commonly referred to as the 'Droeshout Engraving', after its creator, Martin Droeshout, it depicts a middle-aged man with a large forehead, an unusual white collar, an earring and a thin moustache. Droeshout never met Shakespeare so it is assumed that he either copied another picture that was then in existence, or that John Heminge and Henry Condell, the actors who edited the First Folio, provided him with a description from which to work.

There are a few 'problems' with the engraving; the head is large and out of proportion with the rest of the body. Indeed, one conspiracy theorist, Sir Edwin Durning-Lawrence (author of *Bacon is Shakespeare*) has pointed to what looks like a line running down from the ear to the chin, which he believes indicates that the face is in fact a mask, hiding the true identity of the playwright. The collar has also perplexed many scholars; it does not bear resemblance to other collars worn at the time and it looks very solid and flat, with no apparent fastenings, making it likely that it was a product of Droeshout's imagination rather than created through observation.

The 'Chandos Portrait' shares certain similarities with the Droeshout Engraving. The large forehead, earring and moustache are all present, but this portrait also has a beard. The painting's origin is unclear, but the playwright and theatre manager Sir William Davenant may have commissioned it, or been given it by one of Shakespeare's friends. It was owned by the Duke of Chandos before arriving in the National Portrait Gallery in 1856.

A reader who quarrels with postulates, who dislikes Hamlet *because he does not believe that there are ghosts or that people speak in pentameters, clearly has no business in literature. He cannot distinguish fiction from fact, and belongs in the same category as the people who send cheques to radio stations for the relief of suffering heroines in soap operas.*
Northrop Frye, Canadian literary critic

SHAKESPEAREAN SUICIDES

Shakespeare featured 13 suicides in his plays...

Play: *Antony and Cleopatra*
Antony – thinks Cleopatra is dead. Stabs himself.
Charmian – wishes to die with her mistress Cleopatra. Lets an asp bite her.
Cleopatra – grief stricken over Antony's death. Lets an asp bite her.
Eros – stabs himself after Antony asks him to kill him.

Play: *Hamlet*
Ophelia – grief stricken at her father's death and Hamlet's rejection. Drowns herself.

Play: *Julius Caesar*
Brutus – feels guilty over his involvement in Julius Ceasar's death. Runs onto his sword.
Cassius – asks to be stabbed by his assistant Pindarus when facing certain military defeat.
Portia – distressed by her husband Brutus's absence and the strength of Octavius and Antony. Swallows hot coals.
Titinius – grief stricken at Cassius's death. Stabs himself.

Play: *King Lear*
Goneril – stabs herself after poisoning her sister.

Play: *Othello*
Othello – kills his wife Desdemona in a jealous rage. Stabs himself.

Play: *Romeo and Juliet*
Romeo – thinks Juliet is dead. Drinks poison.
Juliet – sees Romeo is dead. Stabs herself.

SETTING THE STAGE

The Curtain

Built in 1577, the Curtain theatre was located north of the London city wall in Shoreditch. Shakespeare's acting company the Chamberlain's Men were resident here from 1597 to 1598 before moving on to the Globe the next year. Manager Henry Lanman, is thought to have helped establish and build the theatre, but by 1627 the Curtain appears to have been destroyed or have fallen out of use as there are no more references or records of it after this date.

SHAKESPEARIAN EXTREMES

Most northerly: Cawdor in Scotland, *Macbeth*
Lying to the east of modern-day Inverness, Macbeth becomes Lord of the Cawdor region at the beginning of the play. It is here that the three witches prophesise that the newly-crowned Lord will become King.

Most westerly: Milford Haven in Wales, *Cymbeline*
Iachimo puts together his plans to murder Imogen in Milford Haven, and it is also here that his treacherous plans are revealed. For Imogen the town represents a sanctuary away from the corruption of Cymbeline's court and the threat of foreign decadence.

Most easterly: Tyre and Antioch in Syria, *Pericles, Prince of Tyre*
Pericles, Prince of Tyre opens in the city of Anitoch where the widowed Antiochus is King. Glorying in the strength of his rule, he manages to rebuff his daughter's suitors by killing them off. Until he is killed by a fire from heaven, he appears to have a divine hold over the noble city.

Most southerly: Syria, *Antony and Cleopatra*
It is in Alexandria that Cleopatra resides in her palace, but the action covered by *Antony and Cleopatra* extends as far south as the plains of Syria.

QUOTE UNQUOTE

Our contention has always been that Shakespeare is our greatest living author. If he can survive a season on Broadway, he must be.
Terry Hands, English theatre director

COMIC TIMING

An Elizabethan comic actor had to be versatile. At the end of each performance he would often be called back onto the stage to sing, perform acrobatic tricks, or dance a jig. Actor Richard Tarlton (1530-1588) did much to spearhead the trend. The favourite court jester of Queen Elizabeth I, Tarlton was so celebrated for his improvised rhymes, jigs and witty stage routines that it became customary at the end of the play for the audience to set him challenges to perform. Such was his skill, he provided inspiration for the playwrights of the time, apparently prompting Shakespeare's depiction of Bottom in *A Midsummer-Night's Dream* and of the court jester, Yorick, in *Hamlet*. Tarlton was banished from the royal court after a scurrilous remark about Sir Walter Raleigh, but a collection of his stage quips and humorous anecdotes were later published as *Tarlton's Newes Out of Purgatorie* (c.1590) and *Tarlton's Jests* (1611).

HELLO AND GOODBYE

The exact dates of Shakespeare's birth and death are not known, but tradition has it that both took place on St George's Day, April 23. The dates are estimates based on Stratford-upon-Avon parish's records, which contain registrations for Shakespeare's baptism (26 April 1564), and burial (25 April 1616). But who else shares this anniversary?

Born on 23 April:

James Buchanan, fifteenth US president (1791)
Edwin Markham, US poet (1852)
Max Planck, German physicist (1858)
Vladimir Nabokov, Russian author (1899)
Shirley Temple, US child actress (1928)
Roy Orbison, US singer (1936)
Michael Moore, Canadian filmmaker (1954)

Died on 23 April:

Miguel de Cervantes, Spanish writer (1547)
William Wordsworth, English poet (1770)
Rupert Brooke, English poet (1887)
John Mills, English actor (2005)

WRITERS ON WILLIAM

To convince you how wretched is the taste which prevails even now in Germany, you only have to go to the theatre. There you will find the abominable plays of Shakespeare being presented, and audiences in transports of joy listening to these ridiculous farces, which are worthy of the savages of Canada. I call them farces because they sin against all the rules of the theatre. These rules are not arbitrary, you find them in the *Poetics* of Aristotle, where the unity of place, the unity of time, and the unity of interest are prescribed as the sole means of rendering tragedies interesting. In the English pieces the action can be spread over years. Where is the resemblance to reality? There are street-porters and diggers, too, who come on stage and speak in a manner suited to their station, and then come princes and kings. How can this grotesque mixture of baseness and grandeur, of buffoonery and tragedy, move or please? One can forgive Shakespeare these bizarre errors, for the arts never come into the world fully grown. But then a play like *Goetz von Berlichingen* is presented, a detestable imitation of these bad English pieces, and the pit applauds and calls for more.

Frederick the Great,
De la Littérature Allemande
The Prussian monarch took a keen interest in the arts and was reputed to be a theatre critic.

JUST BEFORE I GO

Before shuffling off their mortal coil, Shakespeare's characters have been known to voice a poignant phrase or two...

'Now my spirit is going;
I can no more.'
Antony, *Antony and Cleopatra*

'The rest is silence'
Hamlet, *Hamlet*

'Et tu, Brute! Then fall, Caesar'
Julius Caesar, *Julius Caesar*

'A plague o' both your houses!
They have made worms' meat
of me: I have it, And soundly
too: your houses!'
Mercutio, *Romeo and Juliet*

'Mount, mount, my soul!
Thy seat is up on high; Whilst
my gross flesh sinks downward,
here to die.'
King Richard II, *King Richard II*

'Sun, hide thy beams! Timon
hath done his reign!'
Timon, *Timon of Athens*

'I kiss'd thee ere I kill'd thee: no
way but this;/ Killing myself, to
die upon a kiss'
Othello, *Othello*

'A horse! A horse! My kingdom
for a horse!'
King Richard III, *King Richard III*

'Romeo, I come! This do I drink
to thee'
Juliet, *Romeo and Juliet*

*Some, however, just choose to
state the obvious...*
'O, I am slain!'
Polonius, *Hamlet*

QUOTE UNQUOTE

*Think about Shakespeare. It's bloody.
All those things that boys might like.*
Laura Bush, US First Lady, on her intention to use Shakespeare to
educate the ganglands of America

A PUBLISHED WRITER

The following plays were printed in quarto during
Shakespeare's lifetime:

*Hamlet • King Henry IV, Part One • King Henry IV, Part Two
King Henry V • King Henry VI, Part Two • King Henry VI, Part Three
King Lear • Love's Labour's Lost
The Merchant of Venice • The Merry Wives of Windsor
A Midsummer-Night's Dream • Much Ado About Nothing
Pericles, Prince of Tyre • King Richard II • King Richard III
Romeo and Juliet • Titus Andronicus • Troilus and Cressida*

Year, in the 1900s, in which George Orwell's hero, Winston Smith, wakes up with the word 'Shakespeare' on his lips

Outdoing cockfighting for grisliness, bearbaiting was a popular Elizabethan spectacle that would often be slipped into a package of entertainment along with a play and a trip to the local tavern. Human-animal relations were far less delicate than they are now, and tying a bear to a pole with a long piece of rope before surprising it with a pack of marauding hounds was seen as wholesome fare. Of the famous venues that staged such fights, The Beare Garden Amphi-theatre on Bankside was the most prestigious. And of the bears that fought, the ursine Lennox Lewis of his time was undoubtedly Sackerson – a creature famed enough to be mentioned by the character Slender in Act I, scene i of *The Merry Wives of Windsor,* despite the fact the play was set a hundred years before Sackerson was alive: '...I have seen Sackerson loose twenty times, and have taken him by the chain; but, I warrant you, the women have so cried and shrieked...'

The site of the Beare Garden is now occupied by the New Globe Theatre's Education Centre – but its past is still present: a stuffed black bear glowers menacingly in the foyer.

THE AUTHORSHIP DEBATE

Mary Sidney Herbert

In 2004, American author Robin Williams claimed that Shakespeare was in fact a woman: Mary Sidney Herbert, the Countess of Pembroke. The Mary Sidney Society (www.sidneysociety.org) is an educational organisation founded on this premise, arguing that it was due to Mary Sidney's sex that her claims for authorship have gone largely ignored.

The case for:
• Mary Sidney was born three years before Shakespeare and died five years after. She was the most literate, articulate, and motivated woman of her time, and organised a bustling literary society, which wrote many plays and poems.
• Mary was trained in music, medicine, languages, geography,

needlework, alchemy and history. She was also politically involved and frequented the royal court.
• Ben Jonson, widely considered to have been a protégé of Mary's, mentions a mature gentlewoman in his introduction to the 'author' in the First Folio. The publication is also dedicated to her two sons – neither of whom has a proven connection to Shakespeare.
• The Countess had a son who she wished to be married: William Herbert. His initials match the 'WH' to whom Shakespeare dedicated the sonnets, giving rise to the theory that she commissioned or wrote the poetry herself.
• One rumour holds that it was Mary who housed Marlowe after he 'died' in a tavern brawl, and that they wrote the plays together.

Scorsese and De Niro; Corbett and Barker; Monty Python; The League of Gentlemen... sometimes, creative individuals work best in partnership with others. Shakespeare's more affected followers may cringe at the thought, but the creative partnerships of the Bard's time were scarcely any different to the soap or sitcom writing teams of today. These are some of the luminaries who sharpened their quills on his knife:

John Fletcher

A working Jacobean dramatist, Fletcher was keen to work with Shakespeare and wrote a sequel to *The Taming of The Shrew* called *The Tamer Tamed* around 20 years later, to impress him. It seemed to work, as they went on to collaborate on three projects, including *King Henry VIII*, *Cardenio*, one of Shakespeare's lost plays, and *The Two Noble Kinsmen*, published in quarto in 1654, but since dropped from many Shakespearean anthologies, due to the prominence of Fletcher's hand over that of the Bard.

Thomas Middleton

Working as a playwright in London at the same time as Shakespeare, Middleton is thought to have collaborated with Shakespeare on (or revised) the witches' scenes in *Macbeth*. He is also thought to have revised *Macbeth* in 1616 to include extra musical interludes. His modifying hand may have dabbled in a light revision of *Measure for Measure* at some point after its completion.

And *Timon of Athens* is also thought to be a collaboration between Shakespeare and Middleton, which some have used as an explanation of its incoherent plot and uncharacteristically pessimistic tone.

Henry Chettle

A dramatist of Shakespeare's time, many academics strongly believe that Chettle was a co-author of *Sir Thomas More*, a play often attributed to Shakespeare in part.

George Peele

A respected playwright and poet of Shakespeare's time, he is thought to have collaborated on, or later revised, *Titus Andronicus*.

George Wilkins

A member of the King's Men, Wilkins would have worked closely with Shakespeare. He is often associated with *Pericles, Prince of Tyre*, and it is thought that the work was either a collaboration between the two writers, a Shakespearean rewrite of an earlier Wilkins draft, or vice versa.

QUOTE UNQUOTE

*Now we sit through Shakespeare in
order to recognise the quotations.*
Orson Welles, US filmmaker

*Elizabethans used all kinds of public transport
to get to the Playhouse on time.*

A MODERN TAKE ON SHAKESPEARE

Forbidden Planet – A sci-fi version of *The Tempest* (film, 1956)

The Dresser – A story of a Shakespeare troupe whose leader, played by Albert Finney, is trying to keep the group together while playing *King Lear* (film, 1983)

Kiss Me Kate – A Cole Porter musical comedy about two estranged married stage stars who agree to perform a musical version of *The Taming of the Shrew* (stage show, 1948)

My Own Private Idaho – An adaptation of *King Henry IV, Part One* and *Part Two*, following two street hustlers who travel to Idaho (film, 1991)

10 Things I Hate About You – A modernisation of *The Taming of the Shrew* (film, 1999)

Rosencrantz and Guildenstern Are Dead – A play and film written by Tom Stoppard, showing *Hamlet* from the point of view of two of the minor characters of the play (play and film, 1966)

Shakespeare in Love – A fictional account of Shakespeare's life while writing *Romeo and Juliet*. It won seven Oscars (film, 1998)

West Side Story – A musical version of *Romeo and Juliet* with music by Leonard Bernstein and lyrics by Stephen Sondheim (musical, 1957)

POETIC PUZZLERS

Which of these actresses has never played Juliet?
Helena Bonham Carter
Dame Judi Dench
Cynthia Nixon
Vivien Leigh
Answer on page 153.

MOAI FYI

When the steward Malvolio finds a hoax love-letter in *Twelfth Night*, Shakespeare left somewhat of an enduring riddle. Malvolio believes the note, written by Maria in jest, is from his employer Countess Olivia describing her secret love for him, and is overcome with joy. Yet, the note is addressed to the initials 'MOAI' – why?

Popular solutions to the riddle include:

- 'MOAI' are all letters in Malvolio's name. Malvolio himself voices the theory that the letters, once rearranged, spell out his name, indicating the note is intended for him.

- 'MOAI' is a version of the French word 'moi' (me), as pronounced by the English in Shakespeare's time.

- 'MOAI' is a cipher that reversed, represents 'I am Olivia Malvolio'.

TO MUDDY DEATH

**Ophelia's drowning scene in *Hamlet* inspired
several nineteenth-century artists...**

Ophelia (1844)
Eugène Delacroix (1798-1863)
This *Ophelia,* by the important French Romantic painter, is held at the Louvre in Paris.

Ophelia (1842)
Auguste Preault (1854-1855)
This bronze sculpture is now held at Musée d'Orsay in Paris.

Ophelia (1852)
John Everett Millais (1829-1896)
Artist and muse, Elizabeth Sidall modelled for this classic portrait. Legend had it, she nearly died from a fever caught while modelling in the cold bath. Apparently Millais was so intent on the painting that he forgot to replace the candles that were keeping the water warm. The painting is held at Tate Britain, London.

Ophelia (1902)
Odilon Redon (1840-1916)
The French Symbolist's depiction is held at the National Gallery in London.

I suppose the fundamental distinction between Shakespeare and myself is one of treatment. We get our effects differently. Take the familiar farcical situation of the man who suddenly discovers that something unpleasant is standing behind him. Here is how Shakespeare handles it. (*The Winter's Tale, Act III, scene iii*)

> ...Farewell!
> The day frowns more and more; thou art like to have
> A lullaby too rough. I never saw
> He heavens so dim by day. A savage clamour!
> Well may I get aboard! This is the case:
> I am gone for ever.
>
> *Exit, pursued by a bear.*

I should have adopted a somewhat different approach. Thus:

> I gave the man one of my looks.
> 'Touch of indigestion, Jeeves?'
> 'No, sir.'
> 'Then why is your tummy rumbling?'
> 'Pardon me, sir, the noise to which you allude does not emanate from my interior but from that of the animal that has just joined us.'
> 'Animal? What animal?'
> 'A bear, sir. If you will turn your head, you will observe that a bear is standing in your immediate rear inspecting you in a somewhat menacing manner.'
> I pivoted the loaf. The honest fellow was perfectly correct. It was a bear. And not a small bear, either. One of the large economy size. Its eye was bleak, it gnashed a tooth or two, and I could see at a g. that it was going to be difficult for me to find a formula.
> 'Advise me, Jeeves,' I yipped. 'What do I do for the best?'
> 'I fancy it might be judicious if you were to exit, sir.'
> No sooner s. than d I streaked for the horizon, closely followed across country by the dumb chum. And that, boys and girls, is how your grandfather clipped six seconds off Roger Bannister's mile.

Who can say which method is the superior?

PG Wodehouse, *Wodehouse on Wodehouse*

THE LIPSBURY PINFOLD

In *King Lear*, the Earl of Kent says to Oswald, 'If I had thee in Lipsbury pinfold, I would make thee care for me (Act II, scene ii). According to Dr George Weinberg, the therapist who coined the term homophobia, the 'Lipsbury pinfold' refers to fellatio.

THE ROYAL SHAKESPEARE COMPANY

When Charles Edward Flower, a local brewer, donated a two-acre site to the town of Stratford-upon-Avon for the construction of a theatre, he sowed the seeds for what was to become the Royal Shakespeare Company (RSC). The Shakespeare Memorial Theatre (as it was then named) opened in 1879 with a performance of *Much Ado About Nothing*, and quickly gained world renown, adding a month-long summer season in 1910. Disaster struck in 1926, when the Victorian Gothic building was destroyed in a fire, but the festival director at the time, William Bridges-Adams, continued productions in a local cinema, and an international campaign was launched to raise the funds for a new theatre. It was opened in on 23 April 1932, Shakespeare's birthday.

Theatre director, Sir Peter Hall, formed the modern RSC in 1960, changing the name of the theatre, from the Shakespeare Memorial Theatre to the Royal Shakespeare Theatre, in 1961. The RSC has since gone from strength to strength, standing as arguably the most prominent beacon for the interests of theatregoers in this country. The Royal Shakespeare Company's artistic directors have so far included: Sir Peter Hall (1960-1968), Trevor Nunn (1968-1978), Trevor Nunn and Terry Hands (1978-1986), Terry Hands (1986-1991), Adrian Noble (1991-2003) and Michael Boyd (2003-present).

QUOTE UNQUOTE

Shakespeare might have met Rosencrantz and Guildenstern in the white streets of London, or seen the serving-men of rival houses bite their thumbs at each other in the open square; but Hamlet came out of his soul, and Romeo out of his passion.
Oscar Wilde, Irish writer

PERCHANCE TO DREAM

Have you ever dreamt of Shakespeare or his plays?
Well here is what you could really be thinking...

Actor/Actress

To see an actor or actress in your dreams is said to represent a pursuit for pleasure. To dream you are an actor or actress denotes that hard work will pay off in the end. It can also indicate a strong desire to be recognised, or indicate that you are playing a role in your waking life.

Author

To see an author at work in your dream, signifies that your mind is preoccupied with a deep problem.

Writing

To dream that you are writing can signify a need to communicate with someone or with your conscious mind. It can also represent a past mistake.

Number of people The Thistle Hotel's Bards Restaurant in Stratford-upon-Avon can hold, for evening wedding functions, on publication of this book

AN END AND A BEGINNING

*The epilogues and prologues, which introduce
and tie up Shakespeare's plots...*

Prologues

King Henry IV, Part Two, by Rumour
King Henry V, by Chorus before each act
King Henry VIII, no character is specified
Pericles, Prince of Tyre by Gower before each act
Romeo and Juliet, by Chorus before Acts I and II
Troilus and Cressida, no character is specified
The Winter's Tale, where Time explains the passing
of 16 years between Acts II and III.

Epilogues

All's Well That Ends Well, by the King
As You Like It, by Rosalind
King Henry IV, Part Two, no character is specified
King Henry VIII, no character is specified
A Midsummer-Night's Dream, by Puck
Pericles, Prince of Tyre by Gower
The Tempest, by Prospero
Troilus and Cressida, by Pandarus
Twelfth Night, sung by Feste

FROM THE BARD TO BRITNEY

The BBC constructed an elaborate hoax for a Shakespeare-related April Fool's Day in 2004. The story, posted on the BBC Coventry and Warwickshire website, claimed that an academic had traced the family line of Shakespeare through the centuries to pop princess Britney Spears.

The story was 'based' on a re-translation of a paragraph in Shakespeare's will, in which the playwright indicated that he wished his best bed to be left to one 'Bartholomew Mountford', the husband of his younger sister Emily. This couple produced five children, the youngest of which, James, emigrated to America and settled in Kentucky where one of his descendants married a doctor named Spiers. Spiers gradually became Spears, and the line continued down to Jamie Spears of Louisiana, the father of the international popster, Britney. This 'evidence', therefore, concluded that Britney was a direct descendent of Shakespeare's nephew.

It was only when stunned readers clicked to see the proof from the will that they learned the whole story was, in fact, an April Fool.

One of the strangest things about Shakespeare is that, for a man of mystery, he has become remarkably recognisable. And, ever since the Droeshout Engraving immortalised the balding Elizabethan gent we know and love, other artists have created their own versions...

The Stratford Memorial Bust
Holy Trinity Church,
Stratford-upon-Avon
The oldest monument to Shakespeare, this Bust was installed between 1616 and 1623, apparently commissioned in memory of Shakespeare by his daughter Susanna and her husband, Dr John Hall. Centuries of restoration have drastically changed the image to the point where Shakespeare now holds a pen instead of the original sack; an alteration that has given much ammunition to those that don't believe he wrote the works in the first place.

The Gower Memorial
Bancroft Gardens
Stratford-upon-Avon
Presented to the Gardens by renowned sculptor Lord Ronald Sutherland-Gower in 1888, this statue is flanked by statues of some of Shakespeare's best-known characters, including Lady Macbeth, Hamlet and Falstaff.

Bust of Shakespeare
Poet's Corner
Westminster Abbey, London
Designed by architect William Kent in 1740, it was the first sculpture of the poet to be based on the Chandos Portrait. A copy stands in a niche in the wall of Stratford-upon-Avon's town hall.

Statue of Shakespeare
British Museum, London
Created by the French sculptor, Louis François Roubilliac, this statue is on display in the foyer of the new British Library building.

Shakespeare's Statue
Central Park, New York
Built in 1864 to commemorate the three-hundreth anniversary of his birth, this statue stands in Central Park's Shakespeare Garden. The garden also contains 120 plant varieties mentioned in his plays.

Shakespeare's Birthplace
Stratford-upon-Avon
Shakespeare grew up in this half-timbered house in Henley Street. It passed through Shakespeare's descendants until 1806 when it belonged to a butcher named Thomas Court. In 1847 it was purchased by a body of trustees and opened to the public.

New Place
Stratford-upon-Avon
Shakespeare bought this house in 1597 and lived here until his death in 1616. Reputedly purchased for £120 (then a huge sum of money), it was the town's second largest house at the time. Radically altered in 1700, it was bequeathed to the Shakespeare Birthplace Trust in 1891 as a memorial to Shakespeare.

92 *Year, in the 1500s, in which Shakespeare's father John was fined for not attending church*

GIVING A GOOD NAME

Many names crop up in Shakespeare, on more than one occasion. Here are the five most popular...

Five times

Antonio
The Merchant of Venice
Much Ado About Nothing
The Tempest
Twelfth Night
The Two Gentlemen of Verona

Lucius
Julius Caesar
Timon of Athens
Titus Andronicus (twice)
Cymbeline

Four times

Peter
Romeo and Juliet
The Taming of the Shrew
Measure for Measure
King John

Three times

Balthazar
Romeo and Juliet
The Comedy of Errors
The Merchant of Venice

Demetrius
A Midsummer-Night's Dream
Titus Andronicus
Antony and Cleopatra

OH DEER!

Sometime after mid-1584, Shakespeare left Stratford-upon-Avon and made his way to London. But why? The most popular theory, as recounted by biographer Nicholas Rowe, connects the departure with a deer-poaching episode in the park of local landowner, Sir Thomas Lucy. Such was Sir Thomas's anger, recounts Rowe, Shakespeare was forced to flee to London, apparently only stopping long enough to stick his first ever literary piece – an unflattering ballad ridiculing Sir Thomas – on the gate of his property. Later biographers have linked the escapade to the portrayal of Justice Swallow in *The Merry Wives of Windsor*. However no evidence has been documented to back up these stories, and some have even claimed that no deer existed in Sir Thomas's park at the time.

The nasally-exaggerated production of
Romeo and Juliet *went off without a hitch...*

SHAKESPEARE'S CONTEMPORARIES

Michael Drayton

Poet and playwright Drayton (1563-1631) wrote for the theatre between 1597 and 1602, becoming a favourite of the Elizabethan Court and a close acquaintance of Shakespeare in the process. Steeped in the poetry of Edmund Spenser, Drayton's earliest efforts sought to imitate his hero producing a pastoral sequence (*Idea's Mirror*, 1594) and a sonnet sequence (*Mortimeriados*, 1596), which made him a name for skillful wordplay. His *Poems, Lyric and Pastoral* (c.1606) contained 'The Battle of Agincourt', a conflict also covered by Shakespeare in *King Henry V*; while his *Nymphidia, the Court of Fairy*, (1627) was clearly influenced by *A Midsummer-Night's Dream*. The influence went both ways; scholars have found traces of what may be Drayton's writing in some of Shakespeare's plays. Drayton died in 1631, and was buried in Westminster Abbey, beneath a monument inscribed with an epitaph attributed to Ben Jonson.

THE RINGBEARERS

Shakespeare's final act of kindness to his actor-friends was to bestow them with gifts after his death. His Last Will and Testament includes a clause dedicated 'to my fellowes John Hemynges, Richard Burbage, and Henry Cundell [or 'Condell'], xxvj.8. viij.d. [or 26s 8d] a peece to buy them ringes...' It is not known what became of said rings – if, indeed, they were purchased at all.

POETIC PUZZLERS

In the Shakespeare play, who was the merchant of Venice?

Answer on page 153.

WRITERS ON WILLIAM

11 October 1600
Here, in the Park, we met with Mr Salisbury, who took Mr Creed and me to the Cockpit to see *The Moor of Venice*, which was very well done. Burt acted the Moor; by the same token, a very pretty lady that sat by me called out, to see Desdemona smothered.

1 March 1662
To the Opera, and there saw *Romeo and Juliet*, the first time it was ever acted, but it is a play of itself the worst that ever I heard in my life, and the worst acted that ever I saw these people do, and I am resolved to go no more to see the first time of acting, for they were all of them out more or less.

29 September 1662
To the King's Theatre, where we saw *Midsummer Night's Dream*, which I had never seen before, nor shall see ever again, for it is the most insipid ridiculous play that ever I saw in my life.

6 January 1663
So to my brother's, where Creed and I any my wife dined with Tom, and after dinner to the Duke's house, and there saw *Twelfth Night* acted well, though it be but a silly play and not relating at all to the name or the day.

2 November 1667
At noon home, and after dinner my wife and Willett and I to the King's playhouse and there saw *Henry the Fourth*; and contrary to expectations, was pleased in nothing more than in Cartwright's speaking of Falstaff's speech about 'What is honour?'

13 November 1667
To the Duke of York's house, and there saw *The Tempest* again, which is very pleasant, and full of so good variety that I cannot be more pleased almost in a comedy, only the seaman's part a little too tedious.

Samuel Pepys, *Diaries*

Number of coincidences between the works of Shakespeare and Francis Bacon, 95
as cited in Edward D Johnson's Bacon-Shakespeare Coincidences *(1950)*

I saw (or fancied I saw, in the obscurity) a long room with a low ceiling. The dying gleam of an ill-kept fire formed the only light by which I could judge of objects and distances. Redly illuminating the central portion of the room, opposite to which we were standing, the fire-light left the extremities shadowed in almost total darkness. I had barely time to notice this before I heard the rumbling and whistling sounds approaching me. A high chair on wheels moved by, through the field of red light, carrying a shadowy figure with floating hair, and arms furiously raised and lowered working the machinery that propelled the chair at its utmost rate of speed. ..."I am Shakespeare!" cried the frantic creature. "I am writing 'Lear' the tragedy of tragedies. Ancients and moderns, I am the poet who towers over them all. Light! light! the lines flow out like lava from the eruption of my volcanic mind. Light! light! for the poet of all time to write the words that live forever!"

He ground and tore his way back toward the middle of the room. As he approached the fire-place a last morsel of unburned coal (or wood) burst into momentary flame, and showed the open doorway. In that moment he saw us! The wheel-chair stopped with a shock that shook the crazy old floor of the room, altered its course, and flew at us with the rush of a wild animal. We drew back, just in time to escape it, against the wall of the recess... The creature in the chair checked his furious wheels, and looked back over his shoulder with an impish curiosity horrible to see... "Goneril and Regan!" he cried. "My two unnatural daughters, my she-devil children come to mock at me!"

"Nothing of the sort," said my mother-in-law, as quietly as if she were addressing a perfectly reasonable being. "I am your old friend, Mrs. Macallan; and I have brought Eustace Macallan's second wife to see you."

Wilkie Collins, *Law and the Lady*

PATRONS AND PERFORMERS

William Kempe

Included on a list of players who performed in front of Queen Elizabeth I in 1594, Will Kempe (c.1560-1603) was an actor in the Lord Chamberlain's Men, Shakespeare's acting company, and – it is thought – a shareholder in the Globe. Kempe was an actor of comic roles, but he was also reputed to be a great dancer of jigs – an important skill in Elizabethan theatre, which often used the dance to end plays. It wasn't his only dancing speciality; sometime before 1600 (when he recorded it in print), he morris danced over 100 miles from London to Norwich, in an event that came to be known as his 'Nine Days of Wonder' – a misleading title, considering it actually took several months.

A PLAGUE O' BOTH YOUR HOUSES

In Shakespeare's time, the Bubonic Plague caused widespread deaths, with 15,000 reported in 1592 in London alone. Every theatre in London was closed down in 1582, 1592, 1603 and 1608 in response to breakouts. But the connection to Shakespeare ran deeper than that; it is widely believed that Shakespeare lost his sisters Joan, Margaret and Anne, and his son Hamnet to the disease.

Symptoms include fever, headaches, and swellings of the lymph nodes in the armpits, legs, neck and groin. As the disease develops it can also cause bleeding in internal organs, which causes black patches on the skin – hence its nickname, the 'black death'. Without treatment, the Bubonic Plague is fatal, possibly within a few days. It can be treated successfully with antibiotics, but in Elizabethan times treatments usually involved herbal remedies, bleeding, or the use of leeches, which may explain, if only in part, why quite so many succumbed.

FOLIO VS QUARTOS

Technically, a 'folio' is a single sheet folded in half to make two leaves or pages, while a 'quarto' is a sheet folded in half twice to make four leaves or pages. However these terms can also refer to the size of a finished book. A folio is typically bigger than a quarto with a modern folio measuring more than 38cm in height, compared to a modern quarto measuring 23cm by 30cm. Folios were tall, lean and prestigious; quartos were small, square and popularist.

In Shakespeare's time plays weren't considered 'serious' literature, and it is likely that none of his plays would have been printed in folio in his lifetime. Eighteen of his plays were printed in quarto. However, many of these have been designated as 'bad quartos', as the text is significantly different to the 'good' versions of the later Folios. These quarto editions may have been unauthorised printings,

with the text transcribed from the actors' memories of performances of the plays.

The First Folio, entitled *Mr William Shakespeare's Comedies, Histories & Tragedies*, came out in 1623. The second Folio followed in 1632, the third in 1663, and the fourth in 1685. The reissues were based largely on the First Folio, but contained corrections for omissions and mistakes. Only the third Folio carries as much scholarly weight as the First, as it included the hitherto absent *Pericles, Prince of Tyre*, as well as a selection of plays that were subsequently proved not to be the work of Shakespeare. The single-volume collection of Shakespeare's work, now widely known as *The Complete Works of Shakespeare*, has evolved ever since, gaining stage directions and more detailed notes on setting from the pens of later editors.

Some of the places Shakespeare is supposed
to have visited in search of a quick half...

George Inn, *Borough High Street, London*

One of Shakespeare's locals, the George was first mentioned on a map in 1542. It is still a working pub and Shakespeare's plays are occasionally performed in the courtyard.

Crown Tavern, *Oxford*

This was Shakespeare's supposed resting place when travelling between Stratford-upon-Avon and London. Some say that it is here that he had 'relations' with Jane Davenant, the innkeeper's wife, fathering her daughter and the man who would be known as his godson, the actor, poet and playwright, William Davenant.

The Mermaid Tavern, *Bread Street, Cheapside, London*

The chosen haunt of Shakespeare and his contemporaries, 'The Friday Street Club', a literary club also known as 'The Mermaid Club', convened here and counted Sir Walter Raleigh and Ben Jonson as members. It burned down in the Great Fire of London in 1666, but has been remembered in various literary forms, including Ben Jonson's *Inviting a Friend to Supper*, Francis Beaumont's *Mr Francis Beaumont's Letter to Ben Jonson*, and, much later, in Keats' *Lines on the Mermaid Tavern*.

Gray's Inn, *London*

Gray's Inn was one of the famous Inns of Court in Shakespeare's time and was known for putting on shows, including a performance of *The Merry Wives of Windsor* in 1594. As Shakespeare's patron, Henry Wriothesley, was a regular at the inn, Shakespeare probably performed here with his acting company at some time.

The Ship Inn, *Grendon Underwood, Buckinghamshire*

Said to have inspired the rustic humour in *A Midsummer-Night's Dream,* this inn has been renamed 'Shakespeare's Farm'.

THE ORIGIN OF THE BOX OFFICE

Elizabethan audiences of the Globe theatre would place the entrance charge (a penny) in the box at the door to pay for a standing room view of the play. Seats in the first gallery cost a second penny, placed in the box held by the collector at the foot of the stairs, and seats in the second gallery, a further penny, paid in the same manner. Once the play had started, these boxes would be stored in a room backstage, known as 'the box office' (the earliest example of the term). Profits were then shared between the owners of the theatre and the members of the acting company.

Unimaginable it may seem, but we could now have a world without Shakespeare. It wasn't until seven years after his death in 1623, that two actors in his company, John Heminge and Henry Condell, resurrected the original copies of his plays and scratched together the funds to publish them in one authoritative volume: the First Folio. Their enthusiasm, probably inspired by Ben Jonson's publication of his *Complete Works* in 1616, has since proved justified.

Entitled *Mr William Shakespeare's Comedies, Histories & Tragedies*, the compilation was dedicated to William and Philip, the sons of the Earl of Pembroke and Mary Sidney Herbert, Countess of Pembroke. The publisher was Isaac Jaggard, and its contents were registered at the Stationer's Register on 8 November 1623, protecting them in a similar way to modern day copyright.

The edition included a eulogy from fellow playwright and friend Ben Jonson in the preface. It included the following lines: 'To draw no envy, Shakespeare, on thy name,/ Am I thus ample to thy Book, and Fame;/ While I confess thy writings to be such,/ As neither Man, nor Muse, can praise too much.'

Thirty-six plays made it into the collection, omitting *Pericles, Prince of Tyre* and *The Two Noble Kinsmen*. In total, 500 copies were printed, sold for £1 each (around £100 in current money). Only 238 known copies exist today and an original can fetch up to £10 million – so start looking in that attic!

AUTHORED BY SHAKESPEARE?

The Two Noble Kinsmen

The Two Noble Kinsmen appears in some Shakespearean anthologies as the playwright's thirty-eighth play (the remainder generally containing 37). The choice to include or not to include marks an editor's allegiance in the age-old battle between purists and completists: those who believe that only unadulterated Shakespeare should be included in a volume of *The Complete Works of Shakespeare*, and those who think that his groceries list would make a fine addition, even if he collaborated with someone else on it. Of course, for purists, therein lies the problem, for much of *The Two Noble Kinsmen* is the work of Shakespeare's contemporary, John Fletcher. Such is Fletcher's dominance in the writing, the play was dropped from Shakespeare's canon entirely when it was included in a 1679 edition of collaborative plays, by Fletcher and Francis Beaumont, a double-act of considerable renown. Fletcher and Shakespeare are also thought to have linked up on *King Henry VIII*; fortunately it enjoys a somewhat more settled position in Shakespeare anthologies. Not that that's stopped academics from bickering over it.

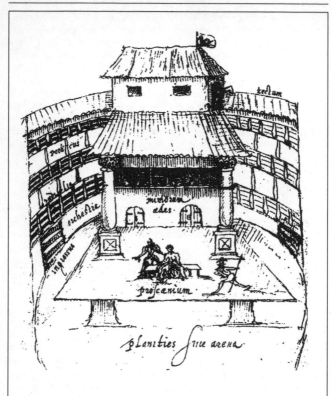

This sketch of the Swan Theatre, produced by Dutch traveller Johannes de Witt, in 1596, is the only surviving representation of any theatre in Shakespeare's London. As well as providing valuable insight into Elizabethan theatrical life, it has recently been used as the template for the reconstruction of the Globe, since most theatres of the time were designed in the same way.

QUOTE UNQUOTE

Shakespeare – whetting, frustrating, surprising and gratifying.
F Scott-Fitzgerald, American writer

100 *Amount, in millions of dollars, made by* Shakespeare in Love *at the US Box Office*

http://shakespeare.palomar.edu/default.htm
'Mr William Shakespeare and the Internet', an online journal.

www.rsc.org.uk
The website of the Royal Shakespeare Company.

www.shakespeare.org.uk
The website of the Shakespeare Birthplace Trust, a charitable
organisation which owns various properties around Stratford-upon-
Avon, including Shakespeare's birthplace and Anne Hathaway's
cottage. The website provides information on Shakespeare's life as
well as the properties.

www.shakespeares-globe.org
Shakespeare's Globe website has information on study days
available for students, as well as information on the current season
of plays being performed at the Globe.

www-tech.mit.edu/Shakespeare
One of many websites with the full text of all Shakespeare's plays.

http://muse.jhu.edu/journals/shakespeare_quarterly
'Shakespeare Quarterly', an online journal dedicated to Shakespeare.

www.pangloss.com/seidel/Shaker
An insult generator that produces Shakespeare-inspired abuse.

www.britishshakespeare.ws
The website of the British Shakespeare Association.

www.bardcentral.com
'The Poor Yorrick Shakespeare Catalog'. A Canadian website
offering an impressive array of popular, obscure, and foreign
language productions of Shakespeare's plays on video and audio.

www.shakespearesociety.org/home.htm
The website for a New York-based Shakespeare appreciation
society. A membership organisation which offers a variety of
educational activities and performances.

www.shakespeareassociation.org
The Shakespeare Association of America (SAA), a non-profit,
academic organisation devoted to the study of Shakespeare, his
plays and poems, and the cultural and theatrical milieu in which he
lived and worked.

www.pbs.org/shakespeare
The official website for the four-part documentary series *In Search
of Shakespeare*, produced by the US Media Company, PBS. It
includes games and lesson plans.

SETTING THE STAGE

Newington Butts

Located in Surrey, about a mile from the Thames, the theatre of Newington Butts stood a long way from London by Elizabethan standards. No doubt constructed out of the centre, to avoid the draconian regulations then placed on theatres in London itself, it is believed to have been in use since 1580 when theatre manager, Philip Henslowe (or James Burbage – Richard Burbage's father – dependent upon the account), stumped up the cash for its construction. It didn't all go to plan; the Privy Council closed Newington Butts and all the other playhouses around London in 1592 in response to a break out of the plague. However, the theatre reopened two years later, the same year as the formation of the Lord Chamberlain's Men. A successful run of performances followed at the venue, including the acting troupe's earliest recorded performances of *Titus Andronicus, The Taming of the Shrew* and *Hamlet.*

POETIC PUZZLERS

**What is the guilty secret the speaker is
hiding in this Shakespearian riddle?**

I am no viper, yet I feed
On mother's flesh which did me breed.
I sought a husband, in which labour
I found that kindness in a father.
He's father, son, and husband mild;
I mother, wife, and yet his child.
How they may be, and yet in two,
As you will live, resolve it you.

Answer on page 153.

SHAKESPEARE IN A NUTSHELL

The Reduced Shakespeare Company (www.reducedshakespeare.co.uk) is a comedy troupe hailing from California. As its name suggests, the Company has made a name for itself by performing *The Complete Works of Shakespeare,* in less time than a traditional performance of just one of the plays. It all began with a break-neck performance of *Hamlet* (lasting 20 minutes) at shows around Los Angeles and San Francesco in 1981. The company then added a 10-minute version of *Romeo and Juliet* to its repertoire, and, by the time it was performing at the Edinburgh Festival in 1987, the show covered *The Complete Works* in 97 minutes.

But how do the company reduce the plays down? Techniques include turning *Othello* into a hip-hop track, performing *Titus Andronicus* as a cookery programme, and combining all of the Histories into a football game.

William Stanley, sixth Earl of Derby

Although it was British archivist, James Greenstreet, who first proposed c.1891 that William Stanley, sixth Earl of Derby, was the true author of Shakespeare's plays, the 'Derbyite theory' remained largely ignored until 1919, when it was revived by Professor Abel Lefranc, one of France's leading literary scientists. He published *Behind Shakespeare's Mask* in 1918, a personal study of the real man behind the name. In it he concluded that the author's first name was doubtless William, but found the idea that this William was the bit-part actor, Shakespeare, ludicrous. He argued that only William Stanley had the experience in the Elizabethan Court to provide the insight reflected in the plays.

As one enthusiast explained in *The Lanciai Free Thinker*: '[Stanley] was closely related to the Royal family and could have become King himself had he wanted to, but instead he wrote *Hamlet* to explain why he declined.'

Finnish scholar Carl O Nordling provided what he considered to be the definitive proof of the theory in 1995. He traced the idiomatic idiosyncrasies of the writing to the northern dialects of Yorkshire and Lancashire, an area home to William Stanley, but one that Shakespeare is not known to have visited. Further proof was presented via a chart of Stanley's international travels. Stanley was once a guest at the Danish Court of Frederick II and the royal court of Navarre, obvious sources for the court scenes in *Hamlet* and *Love's Labour's Lost*; however, it has never been proved that Shakespeare ever left the British coast.

The case against:

Sceptics puzzle why the Earl, if such a prolific writer, left no writing extant under his own name; but Derbyites argue that these would have been destroyed after his death in 1642, Lathom House, the seat of the Stanley family, was destroyed.

D'OH! DOUBLE, DOUBLE TOIL AND TROUBLE

An alternative version of *Macbeth* hit the Edinburgh Festival in 2000, with a cast made up of characters from *The Simpsons*. 'MacHomer' was the brainchild of Canadian comedian and impressionist Rick Miller who recreated the voices of over 50 of the yellow characters for the show. The cast included Homer as Macbeth, Marge as Lady Macbeth and Mr Burns as Duncan. The production kept mostly to the original script, with one notable exception...

Macbeth: 'Is this a dagger which I see before me?
Or a pizza?
Mmmm pizza!'

Total characters in A Midsummer-Night's Dream, As You Like It, Love's Labour's Lost, The Comedy of Errors, Twelfth Night *and* All's Well That Ends Well 103

SHAKESPEARE'S APOCRYPHA

The term apocrypha is given to the collection of 12 plays that, although usually omitted from his canon, some scholars believe to be written by Shakespeare. They are: *Locrine*, *The London Prodigal*, *The Puritan*, *Thomas*, *Lord Cromwell*, *Sir John Oldcastle*, *Arden of Feversham*, *A Yorkshire Tragedy*, *The Birth of Merlin*, *Edward III*, *Fair Em*, *Mucedorus*, and *The Merry Devil of Edmonton*.

SOME SHAKY PHRASES

Some phrases that have nothing to do with Shakespeare...

Shake down • Shake off
Shake up • Give someone the shake
No great shakes • Shake a leg
Shake someone's tree • Shake a stick at
All shook up • In two shakes of a lamb's tail
Movers and shakers • Shaking like a leaf

SHAKESPEARE'S SIBLINGS

Name	Born	Died	What is known about them?
Joan	1558	Unknown	Very little. Baptised in Stratford-upon-Avon. Probably died early, possibly of the plague.
Margaret	1562	1563	Just dates of birth and death.
William	1564	1616	Legendary playwright, but with a past still steeped in mystery.
Gilbert	1566	1612	A haberdasher who worked in London from 1597, but spent much of his time in Stratford-upon-Avon. He died a bachelor.
Joan	1569	1646	Died aged 77, outliving all the siblings. She married William Hart, a hatter, and had four children.
Anne	1571	1579	Just dates of birth and death.
Richard	1574	1613	Died a bachelor at the age of 39.
Edmund	1580	1607	An actor who died at the age of 27. He is buried at Southwark in what was probably an expensive funeral, which suggests that it was paid for by William.

THE ANIMAL WORLD

The animal world is well represented in Shakespeare's plays, which contain references to 180 real and imagined species. Among the nods to birds, bats, insects, rhinos, whales, tigers and mythical beasts, Shakespeare came up with some enduring metaphors...

'A man may fish with the worm that hath eat of a king,
and eat of the fish that hath fed of that worm.' *Hamlet*

'My purpose is, indeed, a horse of that colour.' *Twelfth Night*

'I see you stand like greyhounds in the slips,/
Straining upon the start.' *King Henry V*

WRITERS INSPIRED BY WILLIAM

Said Hamlet to Ophelia,
'I'll do a sketch of thee.
What kind of pencil shall I use,
2B or not 2B?'

Spike Milligan, *A Silly Poem*

SOUND FAMILIAR?

The *Chronicles of England, Scotland, and Ireland* by Raphael Holinshed (c.1529-c.1580) provided Shakespeare with the plots for *Macbeth, King Lear, Cymbeline*, and many of his history plays. Written with the help of clergyman William Harrison and lawyer-translator Richard Stanyhurst, the *Chronicles* are, at best, of questionable accuracy, but still served as a much-used guide for many Elizabethan dramatists. Shakespeare, however, would often borrow more than the plot, as can be seen from this echo in *King Richard III*:

The proclamation ended, another herald cried: 'Behold here Henry of Lancaster Duke of Hereford, appellant, which is entered into the lists royal to do his devoir against Thomas Mowbray Duke of Norfolk, defendant, upon pain to be found false and recreant!'
Holinshed, *Chronicle 72*

Harry of Hereford, Lancaster, and Derby,
Stands here for God, his sovereign, and himself,
On pain to be found false and recreant,
To prove the Duke of Norfolk, Thomas Mowbray,
A traitor to his God, his king, and him,
And dares him to set forward to the fight.
Shakespeare, *King Richard III*, Act I, scene iii

THE FIRST BIOGRAPHER

Although readers often discuss Shakespeare's plays in terms of acts and scenes, Shakespeare's writing originally flowed without such divisions. They were added after his death by dramatist and poet, Nicholas Rowe (1674-1718). Appalled at the presentation of the fourth Folio, Rowe used his knowledge of the stage to divide the plays into acts and scenes. He also indicated exits and entrances, added the dramatis personae to the beginning of each play, and amended spelling and punctuation errors.

Rowe appended a biography of Shakespeare to the edition, writing, 'we are hardly satisfy'd with an Account of any remarkable Person, 'till we have heard him describ'd even to the very Cloaths he wears'. This, the first biography of Shakespeare, included details of the Bard's life, his immediate family and his education, doing much to preserve information that may otherwise have been lost. Rowe credits Shakespearean actor Thomas Betterton (1635-1710) for helping in the research by journeying to Warwickshire to collect items of significance relating to Shakespeare.

OUT OF HIS TREE

Shakespeare planted a mulberry tree, said to be a gift from King James I, in the grounds of his last home, New Place in Stratford-upon-Avon in 1609.

After Shakespeare's death, New Place passed to his last-living relative, his granddaughter Elizabeth Hall. When she died in 1670, the Shakespeare line died with her, and New Place moved into the hands of the Clopton family who had originally built the house in 1483. John Clopton intended to preserve the house as a monument to Shakespeare, but it was sold on his death to Reverend Francis Gastrell, a wealthy Cheshire clergyman, to pay off debts around 1752. The sale coincided with an eighteenth-century renaissance of interest in Shakespeare's life and works, and a steady stream of tourists began to arrive in Stratford-upon-Avon

hoping to visit his house and its famous mulberry tree. Gastrell was none too pleased at the tourists arriving on his doorstep, and, the miserly reverend cut down the offending tree in a fit of rage in 1756. The incensed local community retaliated shortly after by smashing his windows. Soon after, Gastrell fell into financial and legal troubles over land tax demands on the house; it was the final straw, and he razed the property to the ground and fled the town in 1759. It is said that the Stratfordians subsequently passed a law banning any family named Gastrell from residing in the town.

Today the site of the property is owned by the Shakespeare Birthplace Trust and an Elizabethan style geometric knott garden grows where the house once stood.

WASN'T THAT SHAKESPEARE?

Shakespeare was not content to merely languish behind the scenes: he liked to be around, inside and in front of them, too. Here are some of the parts that he is thought to have played in his own works:

All's Well That Ends Well – The King
As You Like It – Adam and Corin
The Comedy of Errors – Egeon
Corilanus – Menenius
Hamlet – The Ghost
King Henry IV, Part One – King Henry
King Henry IV, Part Two – King Henry and Rumour
King Henry V – Chorus and Mountjoy
King Henry VI, Part One – Bedford
King Henry VI, Part Two – Suffolk
Julius Caesar – Flavius
King John – King Philip
A Midsummer-Night's Dream – Theseus
The Merchant of Venice – Morocco, Messenger, and the Duke
Much Ado About Nothing – The Messenger and the Friar
Othello – Brabantio
Pericles, Prince of Tyre – Gower
King Richard II – Gaunt and the Gardener
The Taming of the Shrew – The Lord
Timon of Athens – The Poet

SETTING THE STAGE

The Swan

Francis Langley purchased the manor of Paris Garden in 1589, building the Swan theatre here c.1595-96. Theatrically, its history is unimpressive, with scholars still in debate about whether Shakespeare would have performed here at all, but the Swan does have one infamous claim to fame. It was the theatre that staged Thomas Nashe's *Isle of Dogs*, the 'seditious' play (since lost), which was singlehandedly responsible for the closure of every theatre in London in the summer of 1597. The Swan never quite recovered from the scandal, and although it continued to be used for plays until 1620, it was reported to have fallen into disrepair by 1632.

A contemporary sketch of the theatre by Dutch traveller, Johannes de Witt, in 1596, has provided much of the modern knowledge of what Elizabethan theatres looked like, and academics have theorised that the Globe possessed many similarities to the Swan. Many theatres have been named after it, including the Swan in Stratford-upon-Avon, which is run by the Royal Shakespeare Company.

After his first reading of A Midsummer-Night's Dream, *Tom was away with the fairies...*

WRITERS ON WILLIAM

'I think there must be something in [Shakespeare's birthplace],' said Mrs Nickleby, who had been listening in silence; 'for, soon after I was married, I went to Stratford with my poor dear Mr Nickleby, in a post-chaise from Birmingham--was it a post-chaise though?' said Mrs Nickleby, considering; 'yes, it must have been a post-chaise, because I recollect remarking at the time that the driver had a green shade over his left eye;--in a post-chaise from Birmingham, and after we had seen Shakespeare's tomb and birthplace, we went back to the inn there, where we slept that night, and I recollect that all night long I dreamt of nothing but a black gentleman, at full length, in plaster-of-Paris, with a lay-down collar tied with two tassels, leaning against a post and thinking; and when I woke in the morning and described him to Mr Nickleby, he said it was Shakespeare just as he had been when he was alive, which was very curious indeed. Stratford--Stratford,' continued Mrs Nickleby, considering. 'Yes, I am positive about that, because I recollect I was in the family way with my son Nicholas at the time, and I had been very much frightened by an Italian image boy that very morning. In fact, it was quite a mercy, ma'am,' added Mrs Nickleby, in a whisper to Mrs Wititterly, 'that my son didn't turn out to be a Shakespeare, and what a dreadful thing that would have been!'

Charles Dickens, *The Life and Adventures of Nicholas Nickleby*

SHAKESPEARE ON SCREEN

The first 10 film adaptations of Shakespeare's plays were...

King John (UK, 1899)
This three-minute silent film depicts the death scene at the end of King John by the great stage actor Sir Herbert Beerbohm Tree.

Romeo and Juliet (France, 1900)

Le Duel d'Hamlet (France, 1900)
The first ever film adaptation of *Hamlet,* starring an actress Sarah Bernhardt, in the leading role.

Duel Scene From Macbeth (USA, 1905)
Otello (Italy, 1906)
Othello (Germany, 1907)
Hamlet (France, 1907)
The Tempest (UK, 1908)
Romeo e Giulietta (Italy, 1908)
Romeo and Juliet (UK, 1908)

And the first 10 plays to be turned into films were:

King John (1899)
Romeo and Juliet (1900)
Hamlet (1900)
Macbeth (1905)
Othello (1906)
The Tempest (1908)
The Taming of the Shrew (1908)
As You Like It (1908)
King Richard III (1908)
Antony and Cleopatra (1908)

SHAKESPEARE'S CONTEMPORARIES

Ben Jonson
One of the era's great playwrights, Ben Jonson (1572-1637), was also reputed to be a great drinker; many legends recount the lively debates between Shakespeare and Jonson in the Mermaid Tavern in London. He made his mark as a playwright in 1598 with *Every Man in His Humour,* but disaster quickly followed; he killed the actor Gabriel Spenser in a duel in September that same year, and was imprisoned and sentenced to death. Granted a reprieve at the last moment, his misdemeanour was branded on his thumb and he was released, albeit with his property confiscated. He went on to produce what is generally considered his masterpiece, *Volpone* (1606), followed by *The Alchemist* (1610), *The Devil is an Ass* (1616) and *The Masque of Blackness* (1605).

POETIC PUZZLERS

Match the fool with their play:

1. Feste
2. Trinculo
3. Bottom
4. Fool
5. Touchstone
6. Dogberry

a. *Much Ado About Nothing*
b. *The Tempest*
c. *As You Like It*
d. *A Midsummer-Night's Dream*
e. *Twelfth Night*
f. *King Lear*

Answers on page 153.

WRITERS ON WILLIAM

Mark Twain introduces the few facts recorded about Shakespeare in historical documentation...

He signed [his] will in three places.

In earlier years he signed two other official documents.

These five signatures still exist.

There are NO OTHER SPECIMENS OF HIS PENMANSHIP IN EXISTENCE. Not a line.

Was he prejudiced against the art? His granddaughter, whom he loved, was eight years old when he died, yet she had had no teaching, he left no provision for her education, although he was rich, and in her mature womanhood she couldn't write and couldn't tell her husband's manuscript from anybody else's--she thought it was Shakespeare's.

When Shakespeare died in Stratford, IT WAS NOT AN EVENT. It made no more stir in England than the death of any other forgotten theater-actor would have made. Nobody came down from London; there were no lamenting poems, no eulogies, no national tears--there was merely silence, and nothing more. A striking contrast with what happened when Ben Jonson, and Francis Bacon, and Spenser, and Raleigh, and the other distinguished literary folk of Shakespeare's time passed from life! No praiseful voice was lifted for the lost Bard of Avon; even Ben Jonson waited seven years before he lifted his.

SO FAR AS ANYBODY ACTUALLY KNOWS AND CAN PROVE, Shakespeare of Stratford-on-Avon never wrote a play in his life.

Mark Twain,
My Autobiography

GHOST-TOWN WRITER

If you search for Shakespeare in the index of an atlas, chances are you will happen upon the ghost town of Shakespeare in New Mexico, US. Although evolved from an earlier Indian settlement, the town adopted its name in 1879, when frontier settlers – rich from a mining boom – took inspiration from Warwickshire's most famous resident. This may spark from a slight lack of creativity, but it could have been worse: the residents apparently dabbled with the names Grant and Ralston first.

Once mining wealth had helped cement the town's existence, the town received its fair share of 'wild west' moments. A young Billy the Kid was even supposed to have been working in the town's Stratford Hotel before making his name as an outlaw.

The arrival of the railway heralded the town's decline; it missed Shakespeare by three miles, prompting a sudden relocation of businesses and residents. The town's buildings were bought up in 1935 by a couple, Frank and Rita Hill, who preserved them as well as they could. In 1970 the ghost town was declared a National Historic Site.

RULES ARE MEANT TO BE BROKEN

The 'three classical unities' of drama are derived from Aristotle's *Poetics*, a work that attempted to define the principles of their creation.

Unity of action	A play should have one main action/plot and have no or very few subplots or digressions.
Unity of place	A play should be based in a single physical space and not attempt to compress geography; the stage should therefore not represent more than one place.
Unity of time	A play should represent an action that takes place in 'real time', that is to say approximately the same amount of time as the play – a day at most and certainly not a year.

Only three of Shakespeare's plays (*Othello, The Comedy of Errors* and *The Tempest*) bear any resemblance to Aristotle's principals. Elsewhere the playwright breaks the rules in fairly spectacular fashion: from the 16-year jump between Acts III and IV of *The Winter's Tale* to the wide-ranging locations of *Pericles, Prince of Tyre* and the overlapping plots of *Twelfth Night*. Seventeenth-century poet and playwright John Dryden certainly disapproved of these digressions; in *Essay of Dramatick Poesie* (1668) he lamented the rule-breaking in Shakespeare's Histories, which, in his opinion, 'instead of making a Play delightful, renders it ridiculous'.

Episodes of *Star Trek* to have taken Shakespeare's plays as inspiration...

Episode: 'The Dagger of the Mind' (Episode 11, *The Original Series*)
Source: *Macbeth*
'Or art thou but a dagger of the mind', says Macbeth (Act II, scene i) when he sees a dagger floating before him on his way to murder King Duncan.

Episode: 'The Conscience of the King' (Episode 13, *The Original Series*)
Source: *Hamlet*
'The play's the thing/ Wherein I'll catch the conscience of the king', says Hamlet (Act II, scene ii), hoping to provoke a display of Claudius's guilt through his performance. Kirk mirrors the plot, by unearthing a criminal hiding in an acting troupe by having them perform *Hamlet*.

Episode: 'By Any Other Name' (Episode 50, *The Original Series*)
Source: *Romeo and Juliet*
'What's in a name? That which we call a rose/ By any other name would smell as sweet' (Act II, scene ii).

Episode: 'Wink of an Eye' (Episode 68, *The Original Series*)
Source: *The Winter's Tale*
'Every wink of an eye some new grace will be born' (Act V, scene ii).

Episode: 'Whom Gods Destroy' (Episode 71, *The Original Series*)
Source: 'Shall I compare thee to a summer's day?' (Sonnet 18)
The crew encounter Marta, a patient in a mental hospital, who claims to have written Sonnet 18. 'You wrote that!?' asks Garth. 'Yesterday, as a matter of fact' she replies. 'It was written by an Earthman named Shakespeare a long time ago', counters Garth, to which she responds, 'Which does not alter the fact that I wrote it again yesterday!'

Episode: 'All Our Yesterdays' (Episode 78, *The Original Series*)
Source: *Macbeth*
'And all our yesterdays have lighted fools/ The way to dusty death' (Act V, scene v).

Episode: 'Time's Arrow Part II' (Episode 126-127, *The Next Generation*)
Source: *A Midsummer-Night's Dream*
Trapped in San Francisco, in the 1880s, the crew explain their twenty-third century behaviour by passing themselves off as actors rehearsing a production of the play.

Episode: 'Emergence' (Episode 175, *The Next Generation*)
Source: *The Tempest*
The episode opens as Data performs the *The Tempest*'s final scene. It also introduces characters with names from the play, including Prospero and Miranda.

'There is nothing so dangerous as for one not of our craft to tamper with our freemasonry' wrote Lord Campbell, Lord Chief Justice and later Lord Chancellor, in *Shakespeare's Legal Acquirements* (1859), in admiration of Shakespeare's evident legal expertise. He wasn't the last to be bowled over by Shakespeare's knowledge of the law. Lawyer and Shakespeare fan Richard Grant White supported Campbell's words in his 1865 article, 'William Shakespeare – Attorney in Law': 'No dramatist of the time, not even Beaumont, who was the younger son of a Judge of the Common Pleas,' he wrote, 'used legal phrases with Shakespeare's readiness and exactness... legal phrases flow from his pen as part of his vocabulary, and parcel of his thought.'

White estimated Shakespeare's 37 plays to contain twice the 'legalese' as the 54 plays of Beaumont and Fletcher, giving rise to the theory that Shakespeare may have been a trained, or even practising, lawyer. The theory is of course unproved; but it's a comforting thought to writers everywhere that, after a hard day in court, Shakespeare still had the energy to put quill to paper.

QUOTE UNQUOTE

Shakespeare, in 1595, might have startled us very much, because in 1595 he was not interested in plays, but in poems and sonnets. Highbrows then would have been much more interested in his advances in lyric poetry. It is great luck that Shakespeare had no money and was forced into drama.
WH Auden, English poet and critic

WELL, I'LL BE JIGGERED...

Those who consider morris dancing an anachronism in our time will perhaps be heartened by the thought that it was outdated even in the Elizabethan era; replaced by a new phenomenon known as 'The Jig'. Sometime around the end of the sixteenth century, traditional parts in the morris dance mutated into new characters: the May King and Queen giving way to The Fool and a man-woman figure improbably named 'Maid Marian' (no connection to Robin Hood's love interest has been established). The Jig's visual and comical chaos arose largely from The Fool's attempts to woo the Maid. Whereas morris dancing expressed community spirit, The Jig blew a resounding raspberry at authority – and the stage became its natural home. In its grip, the Playhouses almost lost track of traditional endings: the narrative resolutions of plays would simply collapse into vivid scenes of high farce as The Jig rolled into view.

DID HE REALLY WRITE THAT?

A collection of Shakespeare's most unusual vocabulary...

Baboons, *The Merry Wives of Windsor*
Falstaff: I have grated upon my good friends for three reprieves for you and your coach-fellow Nym; or else you had looked through the grate, like a geminy of **baboons**.

Earwax, *Troilus and Cressida*
Thersites: Here's Agamemnon, an honest fellow enough, and one that loves quails; but he has not so much brain as **earwax**

Pooped, *Pericles, Prince of Tyre*
Boult: Ay, she quickly pooped him; she made him roast-/ meat

for worms. But I'll go search the market.

Dildos, *The Winter's Tale*
Servant: He hath songs for man or woman, of all sizes; no milliner can so fit his customers with gloves: he has the prettiest love-songs for maids; so without bawdry, which is strange; with such delicate burthens of **dildos** and fadings.

While the first three have retained their original meaning, the connotation of the latter example has changed somewhat over the years...

POETIC PUZZLERS

What is the significance of Surrey in *King Richard III*?
Answer on page 153.

THE GLOBE – THE RETURN

The first 10 Shakespeare plays to be performed at the Globe theatre after it was reopened in 1997...

King Henry V – 1997
The Winter's Tale – 1997
As You Like It – 1998
The Merchant of Venice – 1998
Julius Caesar – 1999
The Comedy of Errors – 1999
Antony and Cleopatra – 1999
The Tempest – 2000
Hamlet – 2000
King Lear – 2001

The Two Gentlemen of Verona was actually the first play to be performed in the new Globe, staged in 1996 on a temporary stage the season before the official opening took place.

Sometime during the fifteenth or sixteenth centuries, Middle English became modern English with the dramatic change in vowel pronunciation that became know as the 'Great Vowel Shift'. The Middle English long 'i' (formerly pronounced like the modern 'e') shifted to the current 'i', as in 'high'; the Middle English 'e' (formerly pronounced like the modern 'a') changed to the current 'e', as in 'sheep'; and the Middle English 'u' (formerly pronounced like the modern 'o') changed to the current 'u', as in 'house', in a general movement forward of 'long' vowel sounds in the mouth. But the changes weren't simply limited to a shift in pronunciation; vocabulary and grammar were also profoundly affected by the developing language, in which 'inflectional' endings (the vocal emphasis on word endings, such as the past tense 'ed') largely disappeared. This left the door wide open for writers such as Shakespeare to invent new uses for words, and Shakespeare was not shy about seizing the opportunity, coining such terms as 'tender-hearted', 'dull-eyed' and 'heavy gaited'. He would often use a noun as a verb, an adjective as a noun, or invent 'new' words through the creative use of prefixes and suffixes, or by joining two familiar words to create a then unfamiliar phrase – such as 'arch-villain', 'honey-tongued', 'go-between' and 'well-bred'.

The flow of foreign vocabulary, particularly Greek and Latin, into the English language during the sixteenth century also influenced this trend. 'Neologism' is itself a prime example. It comes from 'neo' (Greek for 'new') and 'logos' (Greek for 'word', as in the 'Word of God').

QUOTE UNQUOTE

There is no argument by which one can defend a poem. It defends itself by surviving, or it is indefensible. And if this test is valid, I think the verdict in Shakespeare's case must be 'not guilty'.
George Orwell, English novelist

DAVID OYELOWO

In 2000, the Royal Shakespeare Company cast a black actor as an English monarch for the first time. David Oyelowo took the lead in *King Henry VI, Parts One, Two* and *Three* at the Swan in Stratford-upon-Avon. Speaking at the time, he said: 'Hopefully it will pave the way for other actors. The more barriers come down the better.' Mr Oyelowo has since played Danny Hunter in BBC One's successful spy drama, *Spooks*.

Number of words in 'Shall I compare thee to a summer's day?' (Sonnet 18)

The worst Romeo ever to disgrace our boards was given by none other than me, *moi-même*. It was to be seen, a bird of ill omen, in Perth during the summer of 1939. I wore a reddish wig (I can't think why), a droopy moustache (a big mistake) and Larry Olivier's cast-offs from the Guilgud production of four years earlier. Pamela Stanley, who had recently made a success in the West End as Queen Victoria, played Juliet and brought to the part all sorts of pretty little Victorian manners; in fact everything except a German accent.

The first night was memorable. I leapt the garden wall for the balcony scene – 'He jests at scars that never felt a wound' – whereupon the wall fell flat. With professional sang-froid I ignored the whole thing and struck a romantic pose of extreme yearning.

But soft, what light through yonder window breaks
It is the east and Juliet is the sun.

At which moment the balcony fell off, to reveal, gasping with aston-ishment, Miss Stanley in her nightie. Another foot forward and she would have tumbled to her eternal rest. The curtain was low-ered. After ten minutes of hammering we started again, to tumultuous applause. The audience was thoroughly enjoying the mishaps, as they always do, but they also wanted, I think, to show their admiration for Miss Stanley not succumbing to the vapours. A few nights later we got successfully as far as 'It is the east and Juliet is the sun' when – no, not so, there was no Juliet. Distant cries for help were heard; she was locked in the lavatory. The curtain was lowered once more while the stage carpenter was sent to release her. It should never have risen again but we persevered. On the last night my ginger moustache got stuck to the phial of poison and after much spluttering with Romeo's last line, 'Thus with a kiss I die', it managed to transfer itself to Miss Stanley's lips. She was not amused.

Alec Guinness,
A Positively Final Appearance

AT HOME WITH SHAKESPEARE

The Shakespeare Birthplace Trust owns for five properties in and around Stratford-upon-Avon, all with some connection to Shakespeare. The properties are: Mary Arden's House, the childhood home of Shakespeare's mother; Hall's Croft, the home of Shakespeare's eldest daughter, Susanna, and her husband Dr John Hall; Anne Hathaway's Cottage, the childhood home of Shakespeare's wife; Shakespeare's Birthplace on Henley Street; and New Place, Shakespeare's last home. The Trust was established after Shakespeare's Birthplace was purchased in 1847, and also owns a museum and library with books, manuscripts and records of historic local interest, with particular reference to Shakespeare.

Find enough clever things to say, and you're a prime minister; write them down and you're a Shakespeare.
George Bernard Shaw, Irish literary critic,
playwright and essayist

SHAKESPEARE ON E-BAY

A search for Shakespeare-related items on e-bay in early 2005 revealed such weird and wonderful items as...

William Shakespeare Cufflinks
Current bid: US$9.50

White Bust of Shakespeare 1:12 scale for a doll's house
Current bid: £1.00

William Shakespeare's Last Will and Testament, Unique!!!
(Reproduction)
Current bid: £9.99

William Shakespeare Brass Ashtray (A brass ashtray with the bust of William Shakespeare on the handle).
Current bid: 99p

Stone from the floor of Shakespeare's School (A small piece of stone which must have worked loose from the floor of the classroom of King Henry VII Grammar School Stratford-upon Avon. It was during a music lesson in the oldest part of the school, dating back to well before Shakespeare's time, where I happened to scuff the small stone loose with my shoe. I picked it up and put it in my pocket and took it home. That was 40 years ago and I've had it ever since. I like to think the young Bard may have walked across that very spot many times during his education and so it may carry the faintest resonance of literary greatness.)
Current bid: 99p

William Shakespeare Rubber Duck (With orange beak that squirts water)
Current bid: £16.65

Shakespeare Action Figure
Current bid: £8.75

Triang Hornby OO4-6-2 'William Shakespeare' Locomotive (Model train)
Current bid: £17.00

Shakespeare Cottage Salt and Pepper Shakers, and Mustard cruet
Current bid: US$24.99

Shakespeare Blend Tea 25 Bags Wood Box (TRY IT!)
Current bid: US$4.50

Rare Sylvac William Shakespeare Toby/Character Jug
Current bid: £9.99

Men's Shakespearean Costume, Renaissance pattern breeches
Current bid: £3.99

ORIGIN OF THE SITH

Star Wars fans know all about the Sith, the evil race who follow the dark side and act as the enemies of the Jedi. But where did the name Sith come from? Some have speculated that the name had a Shakespearean origin, for in his time, the word 'sith' meant 'since', as this extract from *Venus and Adonis* goes to show:

> *What is thy Body but a swallowing grave,*
> *Seeming to bury that posterity*
> *Which by the rights of time thou needs must have*
> *If thou destroy them not in dark obscurity?*
> *If so the world will hold thee in disdain,*
> *Sith in thy pride so fair a hope is slain.*

Star Wars producer and director George Lucas is yet to make comment, but the theory continues to hold weight within many sci-fi circles. They also quote the similarities between the epic struggles of good and evil in Shakespeare's plays, with the temptations of the darkside, in *Star Wars*, as evidence of their theory. However, sceptics quote the existence of Sithonia, an area in Greece, as Lucas's possible inspiration, or, indeed, the man's great imagination – it did, after all, produce the characters of Yarael Poof and Chewbacca the Wookiee.

QUOTE UNQUOTE

Shakespeare once said: Life is pretty stupid, with lot's of hubbub to keep you busy, but really not amounting to much... I'm paraphrasing of course.
Steve Martin, as Harris K Telemacher, in *LA Story*

POET'S CORNER

Part of the south transept of Westminster Abbey, Poet's Corner contains the tombs and memorials of many of Britain's most distinguished playwrights, authors and poets. Alongside the memorial of Shakespeare, you will also find monuments to Lord Byron, John Milton, William Wordsworth, Thomas Gray, John Keats, Percy Bysshe Shelley, Robert Burns, William Blake, TS Eliot, Gerard Manley Hopkins, Samuel Butler, Jane Austen, Oliver Goldsmith, Sir Walter Scott, Charlotte, Emily and Anne Brontë, Henry James and Sir John Betjeman.

Geoffrey Chaucer was the first poet to be buried here. He was followed by Edmund Spenser, Rudyard Kipling, Richard Brinsley Sheridan, Samuel Johnson, Thomas Hardy, John Dryden, Alfred Lord Tennyson, Robert Browning, John Masefield and Charles Dickens.

'Exit pursued by a bear'?, thought Clive, suddenly realising why no one else had wanted the part.

MERELY HELPFUL

An author hailing from Kirton in Lancashire, Francis Meres (1565-1647) unknowingly performed a great service to Elizabethan literature by recording details of poets, playwrights and their work. The *Palladis Tamia, Wits Treasury* published in 1598 compared writers from Chaucer to his own time to classical poets. Shakespeare was compared to Plautus, Seneca and Ovid, and emerged well: 'The sweet witty soul of Ovid lives in mellifluous and honey-tongued Shakespeare', he wrote. 'Witness his *Venus and Adonis*, his *Lucrece* his sugared Sonnets... for Comedy, witness his *Gentlemen of Verona*, his *Errors*, his *Love['s] Labour's Lost*, his *Love['s] Labour['s] Won*, his *Midsummer-Night's Dream*, and his *Merchant of Venice*; for Tragedy his *Richard the 2, Richard the 4, Henry the 4, King John, Titus Andronicus*, and *Romeo and Juliet*.' By including these plays, Meres has helped considerably in the attempt to date Shakespeare's plays; those he mentions evidently written before 1598.

Art – from are, second person singular present form of be: 'Thou art wise', *Othello* (Act IV, scene i).

Betwixt – between: 'The state takes notice of the private difference/ Betwixt you and the cardinal', *Henry VIII* (Act I, scene i).

Dost – from do, second person singular present tense: 'What dost thou mean?' *Twelfth Night* (Act I, scene iii).

Forsooth – literally 'in truth', but often used to express dismay: 'Forsooth, I have forgot', *The Merry Wives of Windsor*, (Act IV, scene i).

Goest – (or any verb ending +est) suffix used to form the present second-person singular of regular verbs: 'Whither goest thou?', *The Merchant of Venice* (Act II, scene iv).

Hast – from have, second person singular present tense: 'Hamlet, thou hast thy father much offended', *Hamlet* (Act III, scene iv).

Hath – from have, third person singular present tense: 'Night hath been too brief', *Troilus and Cressida* (Act IV, scene ii)

Leadeth – (or any verb ending +eth) suffix used to form the

present third-person singular of regular verbs: 'The path is smooth that leadeth on to danger', *Venus and Adonis*.

Shalt – from shall, second person singular present tense: 'Upon mine honour, thou shalt marry her', *Measure for Measure* (Act V, scene i).

Thee – second person singular pronoun: 'If they do see thee, they will murder thee', *Romeo and Juliet* (Act II, scene ii).

Thou – second person singular pronoun: 'I will not eat my word, now thou art mine', *As You Like It* (Act V, scene iv).

Wert – from be, second-person singular imperfect form: 'And for a woman wert thou first created' (Sonnet 20).

Whence – from where: 'Let him walk from whence he came', *The Comedy of Errors* (Act III, scene i).

Whither – from where (destination): 'Sir Thomas,/ Whither were you a-going?' *King Henry VIII* (Act I, Scene iii).

Wilt – from will, second person singular present tense: 'If thou wilt leave me, do not leave me last' (Sonnet 90).

Given the basic nature of the Elizabethan Playhouses, theatre was a province of imagination. Levitating drum-revolves, the like of which were used in a 2005 adaptation of *His Dark Materials* at the National Theatre, were a long way off, and the theatrical experience between players and audience was far more explicitly collaborative. Plays had to be written in ways that would make times, places and actions instantly apparent to the paying throng, as set design was not yet a sophisticated craft.

Playhouses themselves were either many-sided (between eight and 24) or circular, and fashioned from wood, plaster and flint. They comprised three levels of galleries – the highest topped with a thatched or tiled roof known as 'the heavens' – and enclosed an open-air courtyard into which the stage itself extended. A capacity crowd reached about 3,000, and was spread between the galleries and courtyard. The height of an onlooker's vantage point reflected their position in the social pecking order. In high summer, the occupants of the courtyard, usually called 'groundlings', were referred to as 'stinkards'.

A platform stage was between 20 and 45 feet wide, 15 to 30 feet deep, and up to five feet high. Jutting into the courtyard like a truncated pier, it was surrounded on three sides by groundlings, and an appropriate siege-mentality would often take hold: sub-par actors were pelted with whatever rotten matter came to hand, but generally vegetables. Special effects were manipulated from a space beneath a trapdoor in the stage known as the 'hell' of the Playhouse, and there were even trailers, of sorts: flags and banners stationed around the roof that advertised coming attractions, using black for tragedy, white for comedy, and red for history

---

PATRONS AND PERFORMERS

Richard Burbage

The star of the Lord Chamberlain's Men (later the King's Men), Shakespeare's acting troupe, Richard Burbage (c.1567-1619) wasn't just a consummate actor; he was also a theatre manager, the principal owner of the Globe and a major shareholder in the Blackfriars theatre, which he inherited from his father. In his capacity as lead actor, he was the first to play many of Shakespeare's major roles, including Hamlet, Othello, King Richard III and King Lear. Much in demand on the London stage at that time, he also performed key roles for the plays of contemporaries such as Ben Jonson and Thomas Kyd. Short and stout in appearance, Burbage had achieved critical acclaim by the age of 20. His secret? He swore by adopting the persona of the character on stage and off.

The only evidence we have of Shakespeare's existence, apart from the poems and plays, is the portrait of a man who was clearly an idiot.
Martin Amis, English writer

WRITERS ON WILLIAM

When Garrick first came upon the stage, one very sultry evening in the month of May, and performed the character of Lear in the first four acts he received the customary tokens of applause; at the conclusion of the fifth, when he wept over the body of Cordelia, every eye caught the soft infection, big round tears ran down every cheek. At this interesting moment, to the astonishment of all present, his face assumed a new character, and his whole frame appeared agitated by a new passion; it was not tragic, for he was evidently endeavouring to suppress a laugh. In a few seconds, the attendant nobles appeared to be affected in the same manner and the beauteous Cordelia, who reclined upon a crimson couch, opening her eyes to see what occasioned the interruption, leaped from her sofa, and with the Majesty of England, and the gallant Kent, ran laughing off the stage. The audience could not account for so strange a termination of a tragedy in any other way than by supposing the cast to be seized by a sudden frenzy; but their risibility had a different source.

A Whitechapel butcher, seated in the centre of the front bench of the pit, was accompanied by his mastiff, who, being accustomed to sit on the same seat as his master at home, thought naturally enough that he might enjoy the same privilege here. The butcher sat back, and the quadruped, finding a fair opening, got upon the bench, and fixing his forepaws on the rails of the orchestra, peered at the performers with as upright an head, and as grave an air as the most sagacious critic of the day. The corpulent slaughterman was made of 'melting stuff' and, being not accustomed to a play-house heat, found himself much oppressed by the weight of a large and well-powdered Sunday peruke, which, for the gratification of cooling his head, he pulled off, and placed on the head of the mastiff. The dog, being in so conspicuous situation, caught the eye of Garrick and the other performers. A mastiff in a church-warden's wig was too much; it would have provoked laughter in Lear himself at the moment he was most distressed – no wonder that it had such an effect upon his representative.

Richard Ryan
Dramatic Table Talk

Provide an infinite number of typewriters for a infinite number of monkeys, and sooner or later a simian will have bashed out the scripts to any one of Shakespeare's plays. That is according to the Infinite-Monkey Theorem. First popularised by Russell Maloney in his short story, *Inflexible Logic* (1940), the theory goes back much earlier to Emile Borel's work on probability, published in 1909. Since then the idea has cropped up in *The Hitchhiker's Guide to the Galaxy* (Douglas Adams has an infinite number of monkeys ambush the crew for an opinion on their script of *Hamlet*)

and *The Simpsons* (Montgomery Burns fills a room with 1,000 dactylographic monkeys, one of which provides the mistyped 'It was the best of times, it was the blurst of times' as the opening sentence of *A Tale of Two Cities*).

Keen to test the theory in 2003, a group of scientists left a computer keyboard in the enclosure of six Sulawesi crested macaques in Paignton Zoo, Devon for a month. The monkeys first attacked the keyboard with a stone, urinated and defecated over it, and then produced five pages of typing, consisting largely of the letter 's'.

POETIC PUZZLERS

Most people already know that a quote from *The Tempest* inspired the title of Aldous Huxley's *Brave New World*. But what about these other titles, inspired by phrases found in Shakespeare?

1 'the primrose path' (*Hamlet*)
2 'household words' (*King Henry V*)
3 'the sound and fury' (*Macbeth*)
4 'pomp and circumstance' (*Othello*)
5 'winter of our discontent' (*King Richard III*)
6 'in cold blood' (*Timon of Athens*)
7 'cakes and ale' (*Twelfth Night*)
8 'midsummer madness' (*Twelfth Night*)

a Truman Capote
b William Faulkner
c W Somerset Maugham
d John Steinbeck
e Charles Dickens
f Ogden Nash
g Noël Coward
h John Galsworthy

Answer on page 153.

The probable literary sources of Shakespeare's poetry...

The Rape of Lucrece

The original story of Lucretia (Lucrece) is outlined in both Ovid's *Fasti* and Livy's *History of Rome*. According to these sources, Sextus Tarquinius, son of Tarquin, King of Rome, raped a noblewoman called Lucretia who then committed suicide. The ensuing revolt led the Tarquins to be banished from Rome, and consequently caused the founding of the Roman Republic.

Venus and Adonis

The poem takes its inspiration from the mythical Roman characters Venus and Adonis as portrayed by Ovid in his *Metamorphoses*.

The Phoenix and the Turtle

Probably influenced by: Chaucer's *The Parlement of Foules*, which also uses birds as characters; Matthew Roydon's *Elegy On Sir Philip Sidney*; Lactantius's *The Phoenix*; Ovid; and Nicholas Breton's *Amoris Lachrimae*. The poem is commonly thought to be a portrayal of a contemporary relationship. Likely candidates include Sir John Salisbury and his wife Ursula and even Queen Elizabeth I and the Earl of Essex.

A Lover's Complaint

Likely sourced from Poet Laureate Samiel Daniel's *The Complaint of Rosamond* or Edmund Spenser's *Complaints*.

BIRTHDAY PRIZE

The Pragnell Shakespeare Birthday Award is presented every year on Shakespeare's birthday to someone who has made an outstanding contribution to Shakespeare studies or on the stage. Winners include:

1990 Dame Peggy Ashcroft (actress)
1991 Terry Hands (director)
1992 Professor Muriel C Bradbrook (academic)
1993 Peter Brook (director)
1994 Barbara Jefford (actress)
1995 Tanya Moiseiwitsch (designer)
1996 Sir Ian McKellen (actor)
1997 Lady Flower (on behalf of the Flower family)
1998 Sir Peter Hall (director)
1999 Paul Scofield (actor)
2000 Dame Judi Dench (actress)
2001 John Barton (director)
2002 Folger Shakespeare Library (library in Washington DC)
2003 Professor Stanley Wells (biographer, editor and academic)
2004 Cicely Berry (RSC voice coach)
2005 Corin Redgrave (actor)

ALAS, POOR DEL

On his death, actor Del Close (1936-1999), a pioneer of improvisational theatre, bequeathed his skull to a theatre in Chicago. In his will, he stated that his skull should be donated to the Goodman Theatre and 'may be used to play Yorick, or for any other purposes the Goodman deems appropriate'. Close, who passed away on 4 March 1999, had his skull duly presented to the theatre on 1 July of the same year.

WORDS, WORDS, WORDS

Shakespeare is attributed with inventing over 1,700 commonly used modern words. He also changed nouns into verbs, verbs into adjectives, and connected words in new ways. Here are some of the neologisms first seen in Shakespeare:

Bed-room
A Midsummer-Night's Dream
Riddling with words, Shakespeare joined together 'bed' and 'room,' to create the meaning still used today.

Birth-place
Coriolanus

Bloodstained
Titus Andronicus

Cold-blooded, *King John*
Shakespeare hyphenated two words to create a new meaning through their juxtaposition. When originally used, it simply referred to a person who lacked human (warm-blooded) emotions. Today, we employ the phrase to mean emotionless and uncaring, particularly in reference to murder.

Dishearten
King Henry V
Shakespeare added the Latin prefix 'dis' to create a negative version of 'hearten'.

Deafening
King Henry IV, Part Two

Drugged
Macbeth
Shakespeare often took a noun, and turned it into a verb, by placing it in the past tense.

Eyeball
A Midsummer-Night's Dream

Fashionable
Troilus and Cressida

Hob nob
Twelfth Night
In Shakespeare's time, the hob referred to a small projection on the grate of a fireplace, which was used to heat up beer in winter; cold beer, however, was set upon the 'nob', a small table. This would prompt the question: 'Will you hob or nob with me?' Over time the phrase evolved to refer to the social relations associated with the practice of drinking beer.

The Theatre

The Theatre was built in 1576 by theatre manager Richard Burbage in Shoreditch, London. Accounts describe it as being a three-sided timber building, although there is very little information about it in existence. We do know that Shakespeare's acting company the Lord Chamberlain's Men were based here from 1594. In 1599, however, the lease on the land ran out and the theatre faced closure. The company took the theatre apart and transported it across the river where the wood was used to build a new theatre – the Globe.

QUOTE UNQUOTE

Brush up your Shakespeare, start quoting him now,
Brush up your Shakespeare and the women you will wow.
Cole Porter, US composer and songwriter

AUTHORED BY SHAKESPEARE?

For could my worthless brain find out but how
To raise thee from the sepulcher of dust,
Undoubtedly thou shouldst have partage now
Of life with me, and heaven be counted just
If to a supplicating soul it would
Give life anew, by giving life again
Where life is miss'd; whereby discomfort should
Right his old griefs, and former joys retain
Which now with thee are leap'd into thy tomb
And buried in that hollow vault of woe,
Expecting yet a more severer doom
Than time's strict flinty hand will let 'em know...

...Long may thy worthiness thy name advance
Amongst the virtuous and deserving most,
Who herein hast forever happy prov'd:
In life thou liv'dst, in death thou died'st belov'd.
A Funeral Elegy by WS

There was a time when A Funeral Elegy, *written for the funeral of William Peter in 1612, was credited to Shakespeare, prompted in part by its signature of 'WS'. Academic Donald Foster used textual analysis to establish the claim in date; but his theory caused uproar in the world of Shakespeare criticism, as scholars were certain the work was not of Shakespearean standard. It has since been attributed to English dramatist John Ford (1586–c.1640).*

126 *Number of French nobles bearing banners that King Henry V reports are dead in Act IV, scene viii, after the battle of Agincourt*

Improve your vocabulary with the words in the Oxford English Dictionary *that are immediately before and after Shakespeare-related words...*

Shaker *n.*
1. A person or thing that shakes
2. A container for shaking together the ingredients of cocktail etc
SHAKESPEARE
Shako *n.*
a cylindrical peaked military hat with a plume

Barcoo *Adj. Australian.*
Of or relating to a remote area of the country
BARD
Bardot
Brigitte b. 1934. French actress who became a sex symbol in the 1950s and 1960s

Sonic *Adj.*
Of or relating to or using sound or sound waves
SONNET
Sonny *n. coloq.*
A familiar form of address to a young boy

Hamitic *Adj.*
Of or relating to certain Afro-Asiatic languages, including Egyptian, Berber, Chadic, and Cushitic, formerly classified together as a subfamily
HAMLET
Hammer *n.*
A tool with a heavy metal head mounted at right angles on a handle

Macaw *n.*
A large long-tailed brightly coloured parrot native to Central and South America
MACBETH
Maccabee *n.*
A member or supporter of a Jewish family which, headed by Judas Maccabaeus, led a religious revolt in Judea against the Seleucid king, Antiochus IV Epiphanes, from around 167BC, thus stemming the threatened destruction of Judaism by the advance of Hellenism

FAKESPEARE

In 1852, Shakespearean scholar and founder of the Shakespeare Society, John Collier announced he had discovered, in a copy of the second Folio (1632), extensive manuscript annotations inscribed around the time of its publication. 'Tho. Perkins, his booke' was jotted on the outer cover, and the volume became known as the 'Perkins Folio'. His findings, published in *Notes and Emendations to the Text of Shakespeare's Plays* (1853), caused a stir in Shakespeare circles. However, when subsequent examination of the Folio revealed that the annotations were forged in the nineteenth century, an earlier pamphlet, 'New Facts Regarding the Life of Shakespeare, in a Letter to Thomas Amyot' (which Collier claimed to have discovered in a document at the Bridgewater Library), was also re-examined and proved fake – and Collier branded the culprit.

Song: 'Where the bee sucks, there suck I'
Play: *The Tempest* (Act V, scene i)
Sung by: Ariel after Prospero promises his freedom.

Song: 'Fear no more the heat o' the sun'
Play: *Cymbeline* (Act IV, scene ii)
Sung by: Guiderius as a funeral dirge for Imogen who – in a drug-induced state of death – is thought to be dead.

Songs: 'How should I your true love know', 'They bore him barefaced on the bier' and 'Tomorrow is Saint Valentine's Day'
Play: *Hamlet* (Act IV, scene v)
Sung by: Ophelia in her 'mad scene'. The lyrics are all sung to the same melody.

Song: 'Orpheus with his lute made trees'
Play: *King Henry VIII* (Act III, scene i)
Sung to: a troubled Katherine of Aragon.

Songs: 'O Mistress mine', 'When that I was and a little tiny boy', and 'Farewell, Dear Love'
Play: *Twelfth Night* (Act II, scene iii; Act V, scene i; and Act II, scene iii)
Sung by: the professional fool Feste to Olivia; Sir Toby Belch and Sir Andrew Aguecheek; and as part of a drunken free for all.

Song: 'Willow song'
Play: *Othello* (Act IV, scene iii)
Sung by: Desdemona; it was the song sang by her mother's maid, as her mother died after being spurned by her lover.

Song: 'He that hath and a little tiny wit'
Play: *King Lear* (Act III, scene ii)
Sung by: the Fool as he and Lear seek shelter from the storm. It is the only musical interlude in the tragedy.

Song: 'When daffodils begin to peer'
Play: *A Winter's Tale* (Act IV, scene iii)
Sung by: Autolycus welcoming the approach of spring.

Song: 'Under the Greenwood tree'
Play: *As You Like It* (Act II, scene v)
Sung by: Amiens and Jacques as they stroll through the Forest of Ardenne.

Song: 'The ousel cock so black of hue'
Play: *A Midsummer-Night's Dream* (Act III, scene i)
Sung by: Bottom, to show that he is not afraid when he is left alone in the forest. His head just transformed into that of an ass, his singing wakes Titania who, also under a spell, falls instantly in love with him.

128 Line in Act II, scene ii of Julius Caesar, *in which Brutus despairs 'That every like is not the same...', scorning the friends who are planning to assassinate Caesar*

The casting wasn't conventional, but Rupert's Ophelia was a roaring success at his Gentleman's Club.

THE LONG HAND OF THE LAW?

Shakespeare may have made an indelible mark upon literature, but the last remaining vestiges of handwriting that can be linked to him are six signatures on various legal documents. Three of them appear on the pages of his will – but there is a dispute about whether or not they were actually set down by the Bard himself. In his book *In Search of Shakespeare*, the manuscript analyst, Charles Hamilton, who examined the will with powerful magnifying glasses in the early 1960s, contends that the signatures were inscribed by the law-clerk who oversaw the drafting of Shakespeare's will. Hamilton cites an article by Magdalene Thumm-Kintzel in a 1909 issue of the Leipzig journal, *Der Menschenkenner*, in which his prede-

cessor isolated key letters from each signature and printed them side-by-side, proving that the same clerk signed them all. Despite the clerk's efforts to alter the shapes of certain letters as they reappeared (an effect, says Hamilton, of excellent penmanship – or, in other words, an arty streak), the identity of his handwriting is distinctive enough to impose a sense of unity upon the three examples. Hamilton also makes the point that the will was never marked 'signed', but 'published' – a sure indication, he says, that the marks were made on Shakespeare's behalf. The most jaw-dropping conclusion that Hamilton draws from all this is that the man considered the greatest playwright in history was unable to either read or write.

SINGALONG SHAKESPEARE

A Bard Day's Night – The Beatles
Don't Hamlet The Sun Go Down On Me – Elton John
Ot-hello – Lionel Ritchie
Macbeth The Knife – Bobby Darin
Ophelia-ing Good – Nina Simone
Three Times A Lady Macbeth – The Commodores
Ia-go Now – The Moody Blues
Puck Be A Lady – Frank Sinatra
King Lear Of The Road – Roger Miller
Hold Me Titus – Johnny Nash

WRITERS ON WILLIAM

"And you, now, possess Shakespeare's memory?"

"What I possess," Thorpe answered, "are still *two* memories–my own personal memory and the memory of that Shakespeare that I partially am. Or rather, two memories possess *me*. There is a place where they merge, somehow. There is a woman's face...I am not sure what century it belongs to."

"And the one that was Shakespeare's–" I asked. "What have you done with it?"

There was silence.

"I have written a fictional-ized biography,' he then said at last, "which garnered the con-tempt of critics but won some small commercial success in the United States and the colonies. I believe that's all....I have warned you that my gift is not a sinecure. I am still waiting for your answer."

I sat thinking. Had I not spent a lifetime, colorless yet strange, in pursuit of Shake-speare? Was it not fair that at the end of my labors I find him?

I said carefully, pronouncing each word:

"I accept Shakespeare's memory."

Something happened; there is no doubt of that. But I did not feel it happen.

Perhaps just a slight sense of fatigue, perhaps imaginary.

I clearly recall that Thorpe did tell me:

"The memory has entered your mind, but it must be 'dis-covered.' It will emerge in dreams or when you awake, when you turn the pages of a book or turn a corner. Don't be impatient; don't *invent* rec-ollections. Chance in its myste-rious workings may help it along, or it may hold it back. As I gradually forget, you will remember. I can't tell you how long the process will take."

...[H]ope did, irresistibly, come to prevail. I would pos-sess Shakespeare, and possess him as no one had ever pos-sessed anyone before...

Jorge Luis Borges,
Shakespeare's Memory

Elizabethan theatregoers lapped up plays containing sexual innuendo and risqué, often crude, language. Shakespeare was more than happy to oblige...

Impudent strumpet!
(*Othello*, Act IV, scene ii)

And let my spleenful sons this trull deflow'r.
(*Titus Andronicus*, Act II, scene iii)

Our radiant queen hates sluts and sluttery.
(*The Merry Wives of Windsor*, Act V, scene v)

I am one, sir, that comes to tell you your daughter and the Moor are now making the beast with two backs.
(*Othello*, Act I, scene i)

Serv'd the lust of my mistress' heart, and did the act of darkness with her.
(*King Lear*, Act III, scene iv)

One that will do the deed.
(*Love's Labour's Lost*, Act III, scene i)

I have done your mother.
(*Titus Andronicus*, Act IV, scene ii)

Believe not that the dribbling dart of love/ Can pierce a complete bosom.
(*Measure for Measure*, Act I, scene iii)

Come on; tune: if you can penetrate her with your fingering, so; we'll try with tongue too.
(*Cymbeline*, Act II, scene iii)

Use her at thy pleasure: crack the glass of her virginity, and make the rest malleable.
(*Pericles, Prince of Tyre*, Act IV, scene vi)

I conjure thee by Rosaline's bright eyes,/ By her high forehead and her scarlet lip,/ By her fine foot, straight leg and quivering thigh/ And the demesnes that there adjacent lie.
(*Romeo and Juliet*, Act II, scene i)

Am I but three inches? why, thy horn is a foot; and so long am I at the least.
(*The Taming of the Shrew*, Act IV, scene i)

FAMOUS FANS

When Bardolatry took off in the eighteenth century, the stars of the time, including Thomas Carlyle, Sir Walter Scott and Isaac Watts, visited Shakespeare's Birthplace in Stratford-upon-Avon to pay homage to his works. They autographed the walls and windows as a mark of the Bard's importance, and many of the signatures still remain on the windowpanes around the house.

Although all other moons in the solar system are named after Greek Gods, the 27 known moons of Uranus are named after characters created by Shakespeare and Alexander Pope. Shakespeare's are:

Moon: Titania
Named After: The Queen of the Faeries in *A Midsummer-Night's Dream*
Discovered in: 1787
By: William Herschel

Moon: Puck
Named After: From *A Midsummer-Night's Dream*
Discovered in: 1985
By: Images taken by Voyager 2

Moon: Setebos
Named After: The god worshiped by Caliban and Sycorax *The Tempest*
Discovered in: 1999
By: Astronomers Brett J Gladman, Philip D Nicholson, Joseph A Burns, and John J Kavelaars

Moon: Cordelia
Named After: Youngest daughter of Lear in *King Lear*
Discovered in: 1986
By: Images taken by Voyager 2

Moon: Bianca
Named After: Sister of Katherine in *The Taming of the Shrew*
Discovered in: 1986
By: Images taken by Voyager 2

Moon: Cressida
Named After: Trojan daughter of Calchas, in *Troilus and Cressida*
Discovered in: 1986
By: Images taken by Voyager 2

Moon: Ophelia
Named After: Hamlet's love interest in *Hamlet*
Discovered in: 1986
By: Images taken by Voyager 2

Moon: Desdemona
Named After: Wife of Othello in *Othello*
Discovered in: 1986
By: Images taken by Voyager 2

Moon: Juliet
Named After: Heroine in *Romeo and Juliet*
Discovered in: 1986
By: Images taken by Voyager 2

Moon: Portia
Named After: Heroine in *The Merchant of Venice*
Discovered in: 1986
By: Images taken by Voyager 2

Moon: Caliban
Named After: Monster character in *The Tempest*
Discovered in: 1997
By: Astronomers Brett J Gladman, Philip D Nicholson, Joseph A Burns, and John J Kavelaars

Moon: Stephano
Named After: The drunken butler in *The Tempest*
Discovered in: 1997
By: Astronomers Brett J Gladman, Philip D Nicholson, Joseph A Burns, and John J Kavelaars

132 *Line in Act III, scene i of* Romeo and Juliet, *in which an enraged Romeo challenges Mercutio's killer, Tybalt, to fight to the death*

Moon: Prospero
Named After: The sorcerer in *The Tempest*
Discovered in: 1999
By: Matthew Holman

Moon: Trinulco
Named After: The jester in *The Tempest*
Discovered in: 2001
By: Matthew Holman

Moon: Oberon
Named After: King of the Faeries in *A Midsummer-Night's Dream*
Discovered in: 1787
By: William Herschel

Moon: Miranda
Named After: Prospero's daughter in *The Tempest*
Discovered in: 1948
By: Gerard Kuiper

Moon: Rosalind
Named After: The daughter of the banished Duke in *As You Like It*
Discovered in: 1986
By: Images taken by Voyager 2

Moon: Sycorax
Named After: Caliban's mother in *The Tempest*
Discovered in: 1997
By: Astronomers Brett J Gladman, Philip D Nicholson, Joseph A Burns, and John J Kavelaars

Of the remaining nine moons, three – Belinda, Ariel and Umbriel – are named after characters in Alexander Pope's The Rape of the Lock. *The remainder (discovered 2001-3) are all currently awaiting confirmation and naming.*

POETIC PUZZLERS

In the Shakespearean play, who were the two gentlemen of Verona?
Answer on page 153.

PATRONS AND PERFORMERS

Philip Henslowe

Entrepreneur Philip Henslowe (c.1550-1616) built several theatres in Elizabethan London (including the Rose, the Hope and the Fortune) and had links with many others (including Newington Butts and the Swan). Henslowe kept a detailed 'Diary' of his finances from 1692 to 1603, which contains valuable records of performances, takings and payments to the players and playwrights of the day – particularly those of the Admiral's Men, chief rivals of Shakespeare's troupe, the Lord Chamberlains Men. Shakespeare is conspicuously absent from these records, but it wasn't always so. In the nineteenth century, the Diary was in the hands of the Shakespeare scholar, John Collier (later unearthed as a forger), who added Shakespeare's name to the Diary to support his research. It has taken all the ingenuity of modern technology to establish which parts are Henslowe and which are Collier.

Total number of players in King Henry V *and King* Henry VI, *Parts One-* 133
Three – counting up their cast-lists rather than their shared characters

As they read the review for Cuthbert's debut as King Lear, Elisa wondered whether his false moustache had gone unnoticed.

STAGE STRUCK

In Shakespeare's time, the cheapest price of theatre admission was a penny, which bought standing room out in the open yard. The most expensive equivalent was for a seat in one of the boxes over the stage, or better still, on a stool on the stage itself. This fashionable position obstructed the yard audience's view, inviting much abuse. However, it also afforded the opportunity to become more involved in the play. As playwright Thomas Dekker explained at the time (albeit tongue-in-cheek) in *Gull's Hornbook*: 'By sitting on the stage, you have a sign'd patent to engrosse the whole commodity of Censure; and stand at the helms to steer the passage of scenes... you may raile against [the author]... you may happily get you a mistress... you may, with small cost, purchase the dear acquaintance of the boys... And to conclude; whether you be a fool, or a justice of peace; a cuckold, or a captain, a Lord Mayor's son, or a dawcock; a knave or an under-sheriff; of what stamp soever you be; current or counterfeit; the stage, like time, will bring you to most perfect light, and lay you open. Neither are you to be hunted from thence; though the scarecrows in the yard hoot at you, hiss at you, spit at you, yea, throw dirt even in your teeth: 'tis most gentlemanlike patience to endure all this, and to laugh at the silly animals.'

FROM PAGE TO STAGE

Some of the stage directions that cause theatre directors a headache:

The Bear in *The Winter's Tale*

One of the most famous stage directions of all time calls for Antigonus to 'exit, pursued by a bear'. A favourite of pub quiz compilers everywhere, but a bit tricky for stage directors. A real bear is out of the question so directors tend to either go for off stage sound effects or the 'man in a bear suit' look. Some have speculated that because of the Globe's proximity to bear pits in Shakespeare's time, a real bear may conceivably been used. If it was, the part of Antigonus was probably not the most popular with actors.

Jupiter's entrance in *Cymbeline*

In Act V, scene iv a stage directions states that 'Jupiter descends, in thunder and lightning, sitting on an eagle: he throws a thunder bolt'. Which is all very dramatic but not usually that easy to pull off. Legend has it that the original Globe did have an overhead trapdoor and so Jupiter was able to descend in 1611, whether or not on a giant eagle is unknown. These days Jupiter's entrance is usually scaled down to a mere mortal 'enter stage left'.

Macbeth's head

In the last scene of *Macbeth* the violence escalates and Macbeth meets his match in Macduff. Although the end of their sword fight is off stage Macduff reappears, preceded by the stage direction 'Enter Macduff, with Macbeth's head'. Cue the props master and some papier mâché.

The on-stage violence of *Titus Andronicus*

Well known as a particularly violent play, Titus can also cause a few problems for a stage director. On stage a hand is cut off and two necks are broken. But the problems don't stop there as Lavinia also has her hands hacked off and her tongue cut out; not always the easiest thing to mimic on stage.

The gouging out of Gloucester's eyes in *King Lear*

This graphic scene can cause problems for a production as the audience has to see Cornwall remove Gloucester's eyes in Act III, scene vii.

And one casting headache...
The twins in *The Comedy of Errors* and *Twelfth Night*

Shakespeare apparently liked twins and they appear in both *The Comedy of Errors* and *Twelfth Night*. This can be problematic for casting, especially as Viola and Sebastian in *Twelfth Night* are supposed to be so alike that 'an apple cleft in two is not more twin'. Twin Shakespearean actors are presumably a valuable commodity.

The Other Place

The original Other Place (1974-1989), in Stratford-upon-Avon, was a converted tin-roofed storage shed, used as a rehearsal space by the Royal Shakespeare Company (RSC) in the 1960s. In 1973 RSC director, Buzz Goodbody developed it into a small studio theatre, and the Other Place became home to many small scale and experimental productions. It was renovated using the layout of the original theatre, but to allow it to hold an audience of 170. The artistic directors of the Other Place have included: Buzz Goodbody (1974-75), Barry Kyle (1975-76), Ron Daniels (1976-89), Katie Mitchell (1991-98) and Steven Pimlott (1998-2002).

A WILL TO ACT

Sometimes a reputation can take a while to permeate the public consciousness, and Shakespeare's was no exception. One notable sceptic in 1602, namely Peter Brooke, the York Herald of the time, was distanced enough from Shakespeare's achievements to dub him unfit to bear a coat of arms in a registry of 23 'base persons' who he felt had been wrongly elevated to the gentry. This, in spite of the caption on Shakespeare's arms, which read: 'Shakespear ye Player by Garter.' By this time, Shakespeare had already been in the Lord Chamberlain's Men (soon to be the King's Men) for eight years, taking roles in his own plays and those of others. Cast lists included in the 1616 Folio of Ben Jonson's plays place 'Will Shakespeare' in a 1598 production of *Every Man in His Humour*, and 'Will Shakespeare' in a production of *Sejanus* in 1603. It can be argued that Shakespeare's prolific acting in his contemporaries' plays had an inspirational effect on his own. In 1995, subscribers to the internet message board, www.shaksper.net, debated the results of comparison tests carried out on SHAXICON – a lexical database containing *The Complete Works of Shakespeare*, compiled by Donald Foster of Vassar College. The tests found that the roles of Lorenzo Sr and Clement from *Every Man in His Humour* had a strong 'lexical influence' on Shakespeare that filtered through his plays of the early 1600s.

THE OLDER MAN

Rosalind, the heroine in *As You Like It*, adopts the name Ganymede when she disguises herself as a boy. An Elizabethan audience would have got the joke; Ganymede was a young lover chosen by the god Jupiter in classical mythology, and used as slang in Elizabethan times to refer to boys who were 'involved' with older men.

---

136 *One of only two sonnets in which Shakespeare refers to himself, using the name 'Will'. The other sonnet is number 135*

THE AUTHORSHIP DEBATE

Francis Bacon

'Baconians' believe it was Francis Bacon who wrote the plays. This popular nineteenth-century theory hinges on Bacon's legal experience and proximity to the Royal Court, which is said to better explain their composition. The use of the word 'honorificabilitudinitatibus' (the writer's longest word), in *Love's Labour's Lost* is also a contributing factor, for the only other use of this word is found in the collected papers of Francis Bacon, *The Northumberland Manuscript*, in the British Museum.

Sceptics of the Bacon claim recognise Bacon's obvious learning, literary skill and knowledge of the law and court life, but question whether a writer, who already had possessed a busy literary and state career, could have been able to also compose 26 plays, 154 sonnets and two long narrative poems in his free time. Bacon was also alive during the publication of the First Folio – a time when textual problems associated with the text, could have well done with the author's guiding hand.

WRITERS ON WILLIAM

In Shakespeare's room the candles had burnt low. A very tired Master Will was putting down his fifth mug of ale. A very tired Master Pyk was struggling to finish his third.

They were celebrating.

The coaching had taken a long time, passed through many delicate stages, but had ended in a burst of glory with Master Pyk spouting forth words that both were lost in admiration of.

Now they were worn out, relaxed and blissful.

'It is a wonderful play' said Master Pyk sleepily.

'It is a grand play,' nodded Shakespeare.

'It has such gaiety,' said Master Pyk.

'And such poetry,' said Shakespeare.

'Such clowning,' said Master Pyk.

'And such characterization,' said Shakespeare.

They drank.

'One question, Master Will,' said the somnolent Pyk, an idea occurring to him. 'This play – what is the title?'

Shakespeare looked blank. 'Title?' he said. 'Must it have a title?'

'But of course it must have a title,' said Master Pyk severely. 'Have you ever heard of a play without a title?'

Shakespeare considered. His face fell. 'No,' he admitted.

'Then you must find one.'

Shakespeare got up. He yawned.

'It is very late Master Pyk,' he said. 'I am going to bed. Call it what you will.'

Caryl Brahms and SJ Simon, *No Bed For Bacon*

One day (John calculated that it must have been soon after his twelfth birthday) he came home and found a book that he had never seen before lying on the floor of the bedroom. It was a thick book and looked very old. The binding had been eaten by mice; some of its pages were loose and crumpled. He picked it up, looked at the title-page: the book was called *The Complete Works of Shakespeare*.

Linda was lying on the bed, sipping that horrible stinking mescal out of a cup. 'Popé brought it,' she said. Her voice was thick and horse like somebody else's voice. 'it was lying in one of the chests of the Antelope Kiva. It's supposed to have been there for hundreds of years. I expect it's true, because I looked at it, and it seemed to be full of nonsense. Uncivilised. Still, it'll be good enough for you to practise your reading on.' She took a last sip, hiccoughed once or twice and went to sleep.

He opened the book at random.

> *Nay, but to live*
> *In the rank sweat of an*
> *enseamed bed,*
> *Stew'd in corruption, honey-*
> *ing and making love*
> *Over the nasty sty…*

The strange words rolled through his mind; rumbled, like talking thunder; like the drums at the summer dances, if the drums could have spoken… [It] talked to *him*; talked wonderfully and only half-understandably, a terrible beautiful magic, about Linda; about Linda lying there snoring, with the empty cup on the floor beside the bed; about Linda and Popé, Linda and Popé.

Aldous Huxley,
Brave New World

QUOTE UNQUOTE

My goal was very simple: to smash away and tear away this terrible pretension and this very false idea of what Shakespeare is and how it should be performed. I wanted to think about the way Shakespeare would make a movie. He certainly wouldn't make a careful, pretty, framed thing meant for 10 people. He would try and touch as many people as he possibly could, and there would be nothing he would not do in that pursuit.
Baz Luhrmann, Australian film director,
sticking up for his *Romeo+Juliet*

---

138 *Line, in Act III, scene i of* A Midsummer-Night's Dream, *in which Titania, hypnotised by Oberon's flower-drug, declares her love-at-first-sight for Bottom*

In *Brief Lives*, John Aubrey notes that young Will had a go at butchery, as practiced by his father, John. Shakespeare took to the role with a flourish, carrying out all his calf killings in 'high style' and accompanying them with a dramatic flourish. It's a practice that would give any normal parent a sleepless night, and yet, after the business failed in the 1570s, it was Will's earnings that saved the family fortunes. By 1596, John had his own a coat of arms, but how?

Joining the Lord Chamberlain's Men in 1594 would have got Will off to a great start. Make no mistake, this hive of artistic overachievers had a fierce entrepreneurial streak. Taking his share of theatre and performance royalties, Shakespeare invested his money wisely – in property, purchasing New Place and other homes in 1597. As for what kind of money he was making, opinions differ. Shakespeare scholars take one Elizabethan pound as equivalent to anything between £40 and £70 today – a broad margin indeed. Sidney Lee believed William would have made £130 per annum up to 1599 and some £600 later on. EK Chambers accounts annual earnings of £90 in acting fees, £20 as Globe housekeeper, £90 from Blackfriars and Court performances. This would have put him on an annual minimum wage of £205.

There is evidence that Shakespeare's financial health was also the result of money he'd failed to spend. On bills, that is. In an official record of November 1597, he was noted as not having paid taxes from February while living in Bishopsgate. Under various spellings, he picked up two further citations in 1598, and one more in 1599. So it appears that this romantic and poetic force of nature may also have been a common-and-garden tax-dodger.

NOT A VERY NICE MAN

Some of the less palatable events from Shakespeare's plays:

King Lear – Gloucester's eyes are gouged out by Cornwall

Hamlet – The ghost of Hamlet's father recounts how he was murdered by Claudius who poisoned him with hebona

Titus Andronicus – Lavinia is raped by two men and then has her tongue cut out and her hands cut off

King Richard III – Clarence is stabbed by an assassin, and his body is dumped in a cask of wine to make sure he drowns, if not already dead from the stab wounds

Titus Andronicus – Aaron is buried alive up to his chest and left to starve to death

---

Doubts about the authorship of Shakespeare's plays haven't simply been expressed by the odd academic scholar; some of the greatest thinkers have also revealed themselves to be a little on the sceptical side...

In the work of the greatest geniuses, humble beginnings will reveal themselves somewhere but one cannot trace the slightest sign of them in Shakespeare... Whoever wrote [Shakespeare] had an aristocratic attitude.
Charlie Chaplin, English actor

It is a great comfort, to my way of thinking, that so little is known concerning the poet. The life of Shakespeare is a fine mystery, and I tremble every day lest something should turn up.
Charles Dickens, English author

I no longer believe that... the actor from Stratford was the author of the works that have been ascribed to him. Since reading Shakespeare Identified *by J Thomas Looney, I am almost convinced that the assumed name conceals the personality of Edward de Vere, Earl of Oxford... The man of Stratford seems to have nothing at all to justify his claim, whereas Oxford has almost everything.*
Sigmund Freud, Austrian neurologist and founder of the psychoanalytic school of psychology

I agreed to put my name to a school of thought that maintains that the Earl (Seventeenth Earl of Oxford), Edward de Vere, was the author of the plays... Where did this Shakespeare come from? ...I'm pretty convinced our play-

wright wasn't that fellow. This opinion is very unpopular with the good burghers of Stratford, I realise, but they also make their living on the legend of Shakespeare's local origins. I don't think it was him.
Sir Derek Jacobi, English actor

We are The Reasoning Race, and when we find a vague file of chipmunck tracks stringing through the dust of Stratford village, we know by our reasoning powers that Hercules has been along there. I feel our fetish is safe for three centuries yet.
Mark Twain aka Samuel Clemens in Is Shakespeare Dead?

I think Oxford wrote Shakespeare. If you don't agree, there are some awfully funny coincidences to explain away...
Orson Welles, US actor, producer and director

The King James translation of the Bible is considered the greatest piece of literature in English... They say that from 1604 to 1611, King James got poets to translate, to write the Bible. Well, if Shakespeare existed, he was then the top poet around. But Shakespeare is nowhere reported connected with the Bible. If he existed, why didn't King James use him?
Malcolm X, leading spokesperson for the Nation of Islam

PARENTAL WARNING:
TEXT INCLUDES PESSIMISM

Shakespeare's plays have been the subject of censorship over the years, but generally due to their murderous or sexually-explicit characters. In 2001, however, a panel of education experts in the Gauteng Province of South Africa decided to remove the Bard's works from the curriculum for being, well, 'depressing'. They deemed *King Lear* to 'be full of violence and despair', to 'lack the power to excite readers' and to have a 'ridiculous and unlikely' plot. *Hamlet,* meanwhile, was 'not optimistic or uplifting' in any form. Their hitlist also included *Antony and Cleopatra* ('racist and undemocratic'), *Othello* ('racist and sexist') and *Julius Caesar* ('sexist as it elevates the position of men'). The comments caused an outcry and the panel was forced to retract its recommendations.

QUOTE UNQUOTE

Shakespeare was the great one before us.
His place was between God and despair.
Eugène Ionesco, Romanian playwright and
father of absurdist theatre

WICKED WORDS

Shakespeare seemed to enjoy a juicy insult as much as his audience. Here are some of his best jibes:

The most infectious pestilence upon thee!
(*Antony and Cleopatra*, Act II, scene v)

That foul bunch-back'd toad!
(*King Richard III*, Act IV, scene iv)

Thou loathed issue of thy father's loins!
(*King Richard III*, Act I, scene iii)

Thou art a boil,/ A plague-sore, an embossed carbuncle/
In my corrupted blood. (*King Lear*, Act II, Scene iv)

You are a shallow cowardly hind, and you lie.
(*King Henry IV, Part One*, Act II, scene iii)

The plague of Greece upon thee, thou mongrel beef-witted lord!
(*Troilus and Cressida*, Act II, scene i)

You Banbury cheese! (*The Merry Wives of Windsor*, Act I, scene i)

You are not worth another word, else I'd call you knave.
(*All's Well that Ends Well*, Act II, scene iii)

From the most able, to him that can but spell: There you are number'd. We had rather you were weighd. Especially, when the fate of all Bookes depends vpon your capacities: and not of your heads alone, but of your purses. Well! it is now publique & you will stand for your priuiledges wee know: to read and censure. Do so, but buy it first. That doth best commend a Booke, the Stationer saies. Then how odde soeuer your braines be, or your wisdomes, make your licence the same, and spare not... And though you be a Magistrate of wit, and sit on the Stage at *Black-Friers*, or the *Cock-pit*, to arraigne Playes dailie, know, these Playes haue had their traill alreadie, and stood out all Appeales; and do now come forth quitted rather by Decree of Court, than any purchas'd Letters of commendation.

It had bene a thing, we confesse, worthie to haue bene wished, that the Author himselfe had liu'd to haue set forth, and ouerseen his owne writings; But since it hath bin ordain'd otherwise, and he by death departed from that right, we pray you do not envie his Friends, the office of their care, and paine, to haue collected & publish'd them; and to haue publish'd them... absolute in numbers as he conceiued them.

John Heminge and Henry Condell in the introduction to the First Folio

IT'S A DATE

Dating William Shakespeare's plays is not as straightforward as it would seem – *The Comedy of Errors,* for example, is currently thought to have been written any time between 1588 and 1594. The plays that were published in quarto during Shakespeare's lifetime have a publication date, and so can be determined from that. However, the large majority of them were published after he died. Some of these plays are easier to pinpoint than others, as they were entered in the Stationers' Register. This was essentially a list of first-edition works and their relevant publishing dates, acting as a kind of Elizabethan copyright. For plays that do not appear to have any obvious record of publication date, scholars combine the dates of Shakespeare's sources with those of its first recorded performance, to figure out the earliest and latest possible dates it could have been written. However, it is not always as simple as that – for example, Shakespeare and Thomas Kyd both penned, and have recorded performances of, a play named *Hamlet.*

If all these methods fail, experts try to ascertain a date from the style of verse and the number of rhymed lines – often a particular style or influence can pinpoint a specific time in Shakespeare's career. Of course, such vague and varying methods have led to huge disagreements; and for some suspicious scholars, have only provided further fuel for the fires of the great authorship debate.

Line, in Act IV, scene iii of Julius Caesar, *in which Brutus laments, 'Oh Cassius, I am sick of many griefs'*

AT HOME WITH SHAKESPEARE

Shakespeare's Birthplace in Henley Street, Stratford-upon-Avon has been the focus of the town's tourist industry for at least 150 years. In 1852/3, there were 2,321 visitors; in 1853/4, 2,878 visitors; and in 1854/5, 2,436 visitors. The numbers have grown considerably since then...

Year	Number of visitors
1999	510,150
2000	496,576
2001	406,206
2002	383,872
2003	352,501
2004	403,291

THE AUTHORSHIP DEBATE

Christopher Marlowe

'Marlovians' attribute authorship to Christopher Marlowe. They believe the author faked his own death in 1593, before penning the plays under the nom de plume of Shakespeare. The proof? All three of his murderers were on the payroll of Sir Thomas Walsingham, cousin to Sir Francis Walsingham, Marlowe's benefactor. Likewise, the body was never 'found' – it was presumed lost in the number of plague victims, and the death certificate has its share of problems too; it was only discovered in 1925 and is wildly rumoured to be a fake.

Marlovians argue that on Marlowe's death, Shakespeare didn't yet exist as a poet or playwright. Yet, four months after the 'murder', he turns up as the author of his first publication, the poem *Venus and Adonis*. A verse that works perfectly as a continuation of the theme in Marlowe's last work, the idyllic love poem *Hero and Leander*.

In 1900, physicist Thomas Corwin Mendenhall provided further support. He examined the works of 20 authors in a bid to 'fingerprint' their style, producing charts for each author based on their word choice, grammatical structure and style choices. After studying authors, such as poets Shelley and Byron, Mendenhall concluded that it was practically impossible for one author to perfectly mimic another. However, he was surprised to discover that the charts of Shakespeare and Marlowe were identical.

Sceptics of the theory find the falsified death a little difficult to swallow. They counteract numerous borrowings and echoes in Shakespeare's work that support Marlowe's case, by also highlighting the differences in style between the two writers.

SETTING THE STAGE

In Shakespeare's London there were nine playhouses:

The Theatre – built in Shoreditch in 1576 by James Burbage (Richard's father), and removed in 1597 at the end of the lease

The Curtain – built near Shoreditch in 1576, and in use until 1626

Newington Butts – built by Philip Henslowe and/or James Burbage, and in use in the 1580s and 1590s

The Rose – built on the Bankside around 1587 by financier Philip Henslowe, and in use until around 1603

The Swan – built on the Bankside in 1594-95 by Francis Langley, a goldsmith. It was in use until 1620

The Globe – built on the Bankside in 1599 by Richard Burbage, using the remains of the old Theatre. It burned down in 1613 and was rebuilt

The Fortune – built just outside Cripplegate in 1599-1600 by Philip Henslowe and Edward Alleyn as a rival to the Globe. It burned down in 1621 and was rebuilt

The Red Bull – built around 1606 in Clerkenwell. It was in use until around 1663

The Hope – built by Philip Henslowe and Jacob Meade in 1614 in Bankside and designed as both a playhouse and bearbaiting arena. The shape was based on the Swan.

TREK-TASTIC

More episodes of *Star Trek* to have taken Shakespeare as inspiration...

Episode: 'Heart of Stone' (Episode 60, *Deep Space 9*)
Source: *Twelfth Night*
'I have said too much unto a heart of stone', pleads Olivia when declaring love for Violet (Act III, scene iv).

Episode: 'The Dogs of War' (Episode 174, *Deep Space 9*)
Source: *Julius Caeser*
'Cry Havoc! and let slip the dogs of war', shouts Mark Antony as he describes a state of total war (Act III, scene i).

Episode: 'Once More Into the Breach' (Episode 157, *Deep Space 9*)
Source: *King Henry V*
'Once more unto the breach, dear friends, once more', the battle cry of King Henry (Act III, scene i).

Episode: 'Mortal Coil' (Episode 80, *Voyager*)
Source: *Hamlet*
'When we have shuffled off this mortal coil', from Hamlet's famous 'To be, or not to be' monologue (Act III, scene i).

OLD PICTURE, NEW CAPTION

Arguments seemed to require so much more effort since Ethel had been on that Shakespearean acting course, thought Percy.

POETIC PUZZLERS

Untangle these Shakespearean characters:

1. No Mad Seed
2. Rose Prop
3. Hoot Air
4. Stealer
5. Crime Out

Answer on page 153.

EUROPHILE

Shakespeare set his works all over Europe. Italy was, of course, used heavily – Shakespeare, like his contemporaries, favoured locating plays in there, at a time when England was lurching between the Catholic and Protestant faiths. But he also based works in the ancient civilisation of Rome, in Turkey and Greece, and, in Scotland and Wales. Often he chose locations based on the play's source; for example, *Hamlet* is set in Denmark, echoing Saxo Grammaticus's *Historia Danica*, in which the tale first appeared.

Shakespeare first coined 'seven ages of man' to describe a man's progression through life in *As You Like It* (Act II, scene vii):

> All the world's a stage,
> And all the men and women merely players;
> They have their exits and entrances;
> And one man in his time plays many parts,
> His acts being seven ages. At first the infant,
> Mewling and puking in the nurse's arms;
> Then the whining school-boy, with his satchel
> And shining morning face, creeping like snail
> Unwillingly to school. And then the lover,
> Sighing like furnace, with a woeful ballad
> Made to his mistress' eyebrow. Then a soldier,
> Full of strange oaths, and bearded like the pard,
> Jealous in honour, sudden and quick in quarrel,
> Seeking the bubble reputation
> Even in the cannon's mouth. And then the justice,
> In fair round belly with good capon lin'd,
> With eyes severe and beard of formal cut,
> Full of wise saws and modern instances;
> And so he plays his part. The sixth age shifts
> Into the lean and slipper'd pantaloon,
> With spectacles on nose and pouch on side,
> His youthful hose, well sav'd, a world too wide
> For his shrunk shank; and his big manly voice,
> Turning again toward childish treble, pipes
> And whistles in his sound. Last scene of all,
> That ends this strange eventful history,
> Is second childishness and mere oblivion;
> Sans teeth, sans eyes, sans taste, sans every thing.

These roughly boil down to:

> infancy • childhood
> the lover • the soldier • the adult
> old age • senility • death

Or as RM Cornelius put it in *The Rotarian*:

> 6 weeks – all systems go
> 6 years – all systems 'No'
> 16 years – all systems know
> 26 years – all systems glow
> 36 years – all systems owe
> 56 years – all systems status quo
> 76 years – all systems slow

146 *Number of years, after Shakespeare's death, that Louis Francois Roubilliac, who made a bust of Shakespeare for David Garrick, died*

IS THAT A CODPIECE OR ARE YOU JUST PLEASED TO SEE ME?

The codpiece, a favourite of the Shakespeare costumier, was a central part of a man's attire in the fifteenth and sixteenth centuries. It is essentially a flap or pouch that is attached to the crotch of the trousers. How this slightly strange addition to fashion came into being is subject to a few theories. One story believes that the doublet (the cropped jacket of medieval and tudor dress) became shorter to consequently reveal a man's unmentionables. To cover their modesty, men started to wear codpieces ('cod' supposedly derived from 'scrotum'), and the laws of fashion soon determined that the accessory became ever more elaborate and padded. These days the codpiece is generally only seen at the theatre. However, there is one organisation that would welcome its return; Codpiece International (www.users.qwest.net/~rappleyard/codpiece/menu) is campaigning for the return of the codpiece, arguing that it is well overdue a comeback.

THE LORD CHAMBERLAIN'S MEN, INC

Arguably the most prestigious theatre group ever to have gathered in this country, the Lord Chamberlain's Men were a combination of artistic might and fiscal know-how. In less regimented troupes, the notion of the writers, actors and landowners as *bona fide* stockholders would not have been adhered to so strongly, but Shakespeare and co were a tight unit that took things seriously.

Each member of the group, or 'sharer', part-owned its financial and material assets, and was entitled to the appropriate royalties. Shares were also saleable, either to other members of the group or outside interests – the latter sometimes prompted by cash-flow demands. For instance, after the actor member John Heminge died in 1630, his son William inherited his three shares and then sold them on for £506, a sizeable sum.

Although some sharers mingled their tasks, the group was divided, like most businesses, into departments, with some members taking on acting duties, some writing, and others 'housekeeping'. This involved the upkeep of theatrical properties like the Globe and Blackfriars, and the management of profits from said venues. The Globe's original housekeepers were Heminge, Shakespeare, William Kempe, Thomas Pope and Augustine Phillips, who took 10% each, and Cuthbert and Richard Burbage, who took 25% each. And they were evidently scrupulous about banking and insurance: Mark two of the Globe was up and running only a year after the original burnt down in June 1613.

Edward de Vere

A large camp of scholars in Oxford attribute Shakespeare's comedies to Edward de Vere, the Seventeenth Earl of Oxford. It is a view heartily espoused by the Earl's descendants, who refer to Shakespeare, rather disdainfully, as 'that Stratford man'.

The case for:
• Oxford's interest in the drama extended beyond noble patronage. He himself wrote some plays, though there are no known examples still in existence. He also wrote 23 poems in his youth. They ceased just before Shakespeare's work began to appear.
• Oxford may have chosen to assume a pseudonym in order to protect his family from the social stigma attached to the stage.

• Edward de Vere had a 'shakespeare', a man shaking a spear as his coat-of-arms.
• In a 1920s study by J Thomas Looney, *'Shake speare' Identified in Edward de Vere, the Seventeenth Earl of Oxford,* the author highlighted biographical similarities between Oxford and both Bertram (in *All's Well That Ends Well*) and *Hamlet,* and argued that Oxford's poems resembled Shakespeare's early work.

The case against:
A major difficulty in the Oxfordian theory is his death date (1604). According to standard chronology, 14 of Shakespeare's plays, including many of the most important ones, were written after that time.

QUOTE UNQUOTE

I heard that if you locked William Shakespeare in a room with a typewriter for long enough, he'd eventually write all the songs by the Monkeys.
Anonymous

POETIC LICENCE

Shakespeare wrote his first published poem, *Venus and Adonis*, in 1592, when he was 28. He had already made his name in London as an actor and playwright, but the theatres had just been closed after an outbreak of the plague. The closure lasted intermittently for nearly two years, and the playwrights and players would have witnessed a sudden drop in their financial status. Shakespeare was undeterred; he concentrated on making a name for himself as a poet, writing *The Rape of Lucrece*, in 1593, and dedicating it to Henry Wriothesley, Third Earl of Southampton, for which, according to the records of Davenant, he was paid the tidy sum of £1,000.

148 *Line, in Act V, scene iii of* Titus Andronicus, *in which Lucius promises 'To heal Rome's harms, and wipe away her woe!'*

Established by Henry Clay Folder in 1928, the Folger Shakespeare Library in Washington DC contains the world's biggest collection of printed works on or by Shakespeare. He established it as a 'gift to the nation', bequeathing his collection of Shakespearean items, and the money needed to construct the library, on his death in 1930. Its most impressive possession is its row of 79 First Folios – a significant proportion of the known 240 surviving copies. But the library also has a wide range of play bills, paintings, drawings, engravings, prints, musical instruments, costumes and films. The building's north face displays nine scenes from Shakespeare's plays:

Titania and Bottom in *A Midsummer-Night's Dream* (Act IV, scene i)

Romeo and Juliet kissing in *Romeo and Juliet* (Act III, scene v)

Portia (as a justice), Shylock and Antonio in *The Merchant of Venice* (Act IV, scene i)

Macbeth's three witches (Act IV, scene i)

Brutus and conspirators overlooking their victim Caesar in *Julius Caesar* (Act III, scene i)

Lear and his Fool in *King Lear* (Act III, scene ii)

Richard, Duke of Gloucester welcoming the young Prince of Wales in *King Richard III* (Act III, scene i)

Hamlet confronting his mother watched by his father's ghost in *Hamlet* (Act III, scene iv)

Prince Hal and Falstaff in *King Henry IV, Part One* (Act II, scene iv)

SETTING THE STAGE

The Hope

Built by theatre manager Philip Henslowe in 1613-1614, the Hope theatre was located on Bankside in Southwark. The surviving contract for the theatre details its structure, which included a moveable stage and suggests that it was based on the nearby Swan theatre. It was built for the acting company Lady Elizabeth's Men, and as the contract for the theatre was issued only two months after the fire at the Globe, it probably encouraged Henslowe to open another venue in Southwark.

The site he chose was a bear garden and so the Hope was not only a theatre but also a bear pit. The contract stated that bearbaiting would not be put on more than once every two weeks, but bearbaiting proved to be much more profitable than putting on plays. After Henslowe's death in 1616 the impetus to use the Hope as a theatre disappeared and bearbaiting took over almost completely. This continued until 1656 when there were several bearbaiting 'accidents' and the Hope was closed.

The case against... Shakespeare

• Only six shaky signatures on legal documents have definitively been linked to Shakespeare.

• In his Last Will and Testament, no books, papers, or unpublished manuscripts are mentioned, not even a family *Bible*.

• His parents and his children were illiterate, and there is no record of him attending a formal education either, let alone learning the French, Italian, Latin and Greek used in the plays.

• Nothing in Stratford-upon-Avon's parish records suggests he was a writer; he is simply registered as a grain dealer and property owner. And nothing in Shakespeare's writing refers to the town.

• There is nothing in Shakespeare's biography to indicate any travel, legal training or familiarity with international Courts.

• Of the three or four references to the actor William Shakespeare, there is no proven link between the actor William Shakespeare and the William Shakespeare formally resident in Stratford.

• There is no historical documentation to link him to his supposed patron, Henry Wriothesley, Earl of Southampton.

• When the Globe burned to the ground in 1613, contemporary accounts refer to Richard Burbage, Henry Condell and other Globe officials, but nothing is said about Shakespeare.

• When Shakespeare died in 1616, no eulogies were published.

The first eulogy didn't appear until the First Folio of 1623.

• On Shakespeare's death, many of the plays attributed to him had yet to be published. The First Folio included 16 hitherto unprinted works. And anti-Stratfordian's also argue that many of these were yet to have been performed (or even written). Likewise, there are a number of 'apocryphal' plays, which match Shakespeare's writing style exactly, and yet have been ruled out of the playwright's canon because they date to a time when Shakespeare could not possibly have written them.

• The monument to Shakespeare in Stratford-upon-Avon's Holy Trinity Church originally showed a man holding a sack, not a man writing on a pillow.

• Shakespeare's daughter, Susanna, inherited the estate. Yet, she never claimed any ownership over or financial reward from the First Folio.

• The Elizabethan actor, Edward Alleyn, noted in his diaries the names of all the actors and dramatists of his time, and those connected with the production of plays at the Fortune, Blackfriars, and other theatres. Shakespeare is not mentioned once.

• Henslowe's theatrical diary mentions Shakespeare's plays, but not Shakespeare himself, leading to the conclusion that Henslowe never paid anyone named Shakespeare for his plays.

DURING THE COMPILATION OF THIS BOOK, THE COMPANION TEAM...

Re-enacted the entire canon of Shakespeare's plays using only a packet of salt and vinegar crisps, a packet of honey-roasted peanuts and three beer mats

Used the word 'forsooth', in entirely inappropriate situations, eight times

Saw three stage productions and eight film adaptations of Shakespeare's plays, and also overheard a bloke on the bus misquote a line from *Macbeth* on his mobile

Named their new pair of pet goldfish Troilus and Cressida

Spent 7.1 hours convincing themselves that visiting the Shakespeare's Head pub round the corner counted as 'research'

Composed 43 completely rubbish sonnets, 62% of which didn't rhyme properly and 86% were too rude to show anyone anyway

Spent 9.1 hours checking they didn't have the plague

Went to three fancy dress parties they weren't invited to, but on every single occasion completely failed to meet the love of their life while looking through a fish tank

Relieved 16 geese of feathers to make quills, but couldn't work out how to write anything coherently

Spent 4.614 hours rehearsing their 'To be or not to be' soliloquy, only to be laughed out of the office during their first public performance

Realised that none of their friends knew that Shakespeare had written a play called *Cymbeline*

Attended the funeral of the short-lived, but much missed, Troilus the goldfish. (But then bought two more, and called them Rosencrantz and Guildenstern)

Please note that although every effort has been made to ensure accuracy in this book, the above statistics may be the result of over-scripted minds.

*Shakespeare had no tutors
but nature and genius.*

Horace Walpole

The answers. As if you needed them.

P12.   Ephesus is the odd one out. All four are used by Shakespeare
       as locations for his plays, but Ephesus (in *The Comedy of
       Errors*) no longer exists. Its ruins stand in a village in Turkey.

P24.   Kenneth Branagh

P31.   1. Cordelia (*King Lear*)
       2. Ophelia (*Hamlet*)
       3. Cleopatra (*Antony and Cleopatra*)
       4. Coriolanus (*Coriolanus*)
       5. Petruchio (*The Taming of the Shrew*)

P41.   1. *Julius Caesar*
       2. *The Merchant of Venice*
       3. *Much Ado About Nothing*
       4. *The Two Gentlemen of Verona*
       5. *King Henry VI, Part One*
       6. *Love's Labour's Lost*
       7. *Othello*
       8. *The Comedy of Errors*

P46.   Sir Anthony Hopkins

P54.   1. *Twelfth Night*
       2. *King Lear*
       3. *Romeo and Juliet*
       4. *Measure for Measure*
       5. King *Richard II*
       6. *Much Ado About Nothing*
       7. *The Tempest*
       8. *Coriolanus*

P65.   Navarre is the odd one out. All four are used by
       Shakespeare as locations for his plays, but Navarre
       (in *Love's Labour's Lost*) no longer exists. It is now
       a province of Spain.

P66.   1. *Antony and Cleopatra*
       2. *A Midsummer-Night's Dream*
       3. *Timon of Athens*
       4. *Measure for Measure*
       5. *Hamlet*
       6. *King John*
       7. *The Winter's Tale*

P78.   Lynne Redgrave

P88.   Helena Bonham Carter

P95.   Antonio

P102. An incestuous relationship. In the opening scene of *Pericles, Prince of Tyre* the hero must answer the riddle correctly to marry Antiochus's daughter. If he fails to answer the riddle correctly he will be killed, but – as the answer is incest – if he reveals the truth, he will also be killed. Instead of answering outright the hero instead hints at the answer, but asks for more time to think. He is granted 40 days and uses the time to flee Antioch.

P110. Feste, *Twelfth Night*
Trinculo, *The Tempest*
Bottom, *A Midsummer-Night's Dream*
Fool, *King Lear*
Touchstone, *As You Like It*
Dogberry, *Much Ado About Nothing*

P114. Surrey is Richard's horse

P123. 1. 'The primrose path' – f. Ogden Nash
2. 'Household words' – e. Charles Dickens
3. 'Sound and fury' – b William Faulkner
4. 'Pomp and circumstance' – g. Noel Coward
5. 'Winter of our discontent' – d. John Steinbeck
6. 'In cold blood' – a. Truman Capote
7. 'Cakes and ale' – c. W Somerset Maugham
8. 'Midsummer madness' – h. John Galsworthy

P133. Valentine and Proteus

P145. 1. Desdemona (*Othello*)
2. Prospero (*The Tempest*)
3. Horatio (*Hamlet*)
4. Laertes (*Hamlet*)
5. Mercutio (*Romeo and Juliet*)

After Shakespeare, John Gross

The Cambridge Companion to Shakespeare,
Margreta De Grazia and Stanley Wells

The Complete Works of Shakespeare, The Alexander Text

The Concise Oxford Dictionary of Quotations

A Dictionary of Who, What and Where in Shakespeare,
Royal Shakespeare Company

The Methuen Book of Shakespeare Anecdotes, Ralph Berry

Naughty Shakespeare, Michael Macrone

Shakespeare's Insults, Wayne F Hill and Cynthia J Ottchen

The Shakespeare Name Dictionary, J Madison Davis
and A Daniel Frankforter

Shakespeare's Names, Louis Colaianni

The Top 100 of Everything, Russell Ash

Is this the promis'd end?

King Lear, Act V, scene iii

Line in Act IV, scene i of The Tempest, *in which Prospero starts to deliver the famous words, 'We are such stuff/ As dreams are made on...'*

ACKNOWLEDGEMENTS

We gratefully acknowledge permission to reprint extracts of copyright material in this book from the following authors, publishers and executors:

'The Immortal Bard', copyright 1953 by Palmer Publications, Inc., from *Earth Is Room Enough* by Isaac Asimov. Used by permission of Doubleday, a division of Random House, Inc.

Shakespeare's Memory by Jorge Luis Borges Copyright © Maria Kodama 1998. Reprinted by permission of the Wylie Agency (UK) Ltd.

No Bed for Bacon by Caryl Brahms and SJ Simon, reproduced by kind permission of Ned Sherrin.

My Autobiography by Charles Chaplin, published by The Bodley Head. Reprinted by permission of The Random House Group Ltd.

A Positively Final Appearance by Alec Guinness (Hamish Hamilton, 1999). Copyright © Alec Guinness, 1999

Brave New World by Aldous Huxley, reproduced by kind permission of the Reece Halsey Agency.

Shakespeare is Hard, But So Is Life by Fintan O'Toole, reproduced by permission of AP Watt Ltd on behalf of Fintan O'Toole.

Wodehouse on Wodehouse by PG Wodehouse, published by Hutchinson. Reprinted by permission of The Random House Group Ltd.
Wodehouse on Wodehouse by PG Wodehouse, reproduced by permission of AP Watt on behalf of The Trustees of the Wodehouse Estate.

Anagrams on page 56, thanks to Cory Calhoun, and Anagram Genius (www.anagramgenius.com) and its contributors.

Amount, in tens of thousands of dollars, grossed at the US Box Office in the year 2000 by Michael Almereyda's film of Hamlet, starring Ethan Hawke 157

INDEX

FILL YOUR BOOKSHELF AND YOUR MIND

The Birdwatcher's Companion Twitchers, birders and ornithologists are all catered for in this unique book. ISBN 1-86105-833-0

The Cook's Companion Foie gras or fry-ups, this tasty compilation is an essential ingredient in any kitchen. ISBN 1-86105-772-5

The Countryside Companion From milking stools to crofters tools, this book opens the lid on the rural scene. ISBN 1-86105-918-3

The Fishing Companion This fascinating catch of fishy facts offers a whole new angle on angling. ISBN 1-86105-919-1

The Gardener's Companion For anyone who has ever gone in search of flowers, beauty and inspiration. ISBN 1-86105-771-7

The Golfer's Companion From plus fours to six irons, here's where to find the heaven and hell of golf. ISBN 1-86105-834-9

The History of Britain Companion All the oddities, quirks, origins and stories that make our country what it is today. ISBN 1-86105-914-0

The Ideas Companion The stories behind the trademarks, inventions, and brands that we come across every day. ISBN 1-86105-835-7

The Legal Companion From lawmakers to lawbreakers, find out all the quirks and stories behind the legal world. ISBN 1-86105-838-1

The Literary Companion Literary fact and fiction from Rebecca East to Vita Sackville-West. ISBN 1-86105-798-9

The London Companion Explore the history and mystery of the most exciting capital city in the world. ISBN 1-86105-799-7

The Moviegoer's Companion Movies, actors, cinemas and salty popcorn in all their glamorous glory. ISBN 1-86105-797-0

The Politics Companion Great leaders and greater liars of international politics gather round the hustings. ISBN 1-86105-796-2

The Sailing Companion Starboards, stinkpots, raggie and sterns – here's where to find out more. ISBN 1-86105-839-X

The Shakespeare Companion A long, hard look at the man behind the moustache and his plethora of works. ISBN 1-86105-913-2

The Traveller's Companion For anyone who's ever stared at a plane and spent the day dreaming of faraway lands. ISBN 1-86105-773-3

The Walker's Companion Ever laced a sturdy boot and stepped out in search of stimulation? This book is for you. ISBN 1-86105-825-X

The Wildlife Companion Animal amazements and botanical beauties abound in this book of natural need-to-knows. ISBN 1-86105-770-9